A WISCONSIN TRAILS GUIDE

# GREAT GOLF IN WISCONSIN

BY JOHN HUGHES AND JEFF MAYERS

Published by Wisconsin Trails

First Edition, First Printing
Copyright © 1994 by Wisconsin Trails
Text Copyright © by John Hughes and Jeff Mayers
Cover Photograph, Trappers Turn by Craig Benson

All rights reserved. No part of this publication may be reproduced or transmitted in any form or by any means, electronic or mechanical, including photocopy, recording or any information storage retrieval system, without permission in writing from the publisher.

Wisconsin Trails
P.O. Box 5650 • 6225 University Avenue
Madison, Wisconsin 53705
(608) 231-2444   FAX (608) 231-1557

Library of Congress Catalog Card Number: 94-60729

ISBN 0-915024-43-8

Design by Kathie Campbell
Printing by BookCrafters • Chelsea, Michigan

Printed in the United States of America
First Printing May 1994

# Introduction

By John Hughes and Jeff Mayers

When you think of golf, your first thoughts might be of Florida, Arizona, Hawaii and North Carolina, and it's true those are fine golfing states. But unless you consider Wisconsin among the great places to golf you're not seeing the entire picture.

As a result of our enviable travels around the state collecting information for this book, we can say with certainty that Wisconsin has a remarkable variety of outstanding golf courses. There are good courses, and great courses, from virtually all the master designers, including Donald Ross, Robert Trent Jones, Pete Dye and Jack Nicklaus. There are courses perfectly suited to the person who plays league golf or goes out for the nine-hole round after work, and courses that will test the skill of a low-handicap player.

With more than 336 courses in the state open to the public (and more being built every year), we can claim that there's something for everyone when it comes to golfing in Wisconsin.

The road trips we took in the name of "research" brought us from Lake Geneva to Rhinelander, from Spring Green to Door County and many points in between. Along the way we found the joy that only a footloose golfer could find.

Got up. Checked the weather. Picked a course. And hit the road, to discover new fairways. The golf was never disappointing, although the scores often were.

On the way home, we'd stop for a bite to eat. Not at a five-star restaurant, but a family eatery where a meat loaf sandwich might be the special of the day.

With Wisconsin's green countryside as the backdrop, we'd exchange stories, listen to the sounds of summer baseball on the radio, and chew over the difficulties of perfecting our imperfect swings.

Playing this grand game, we realized, was what a lot of people do in Wisconsin in the summertime. That thought only bolstered our belief that a guide book to Wisconsin golf could help others experience the joy of finding a new course in a pretty place.

Our goal here was to take some of the guesswork out of the search. In this book we feature 25 of Wisconsin's elite public courses, mixing course descriptions, history, the feel of the courses, and the challenges to anticipate.

In addition, we have compiled a list of regulation public courses throughout the state, with information telling you how to get there and what you'll find upon your arrival. The list is as complete as we could make it.

We hope our book helps you enjoy Wisconsin golf as much as we do. ☐

# Locations of the 25 Best Courses

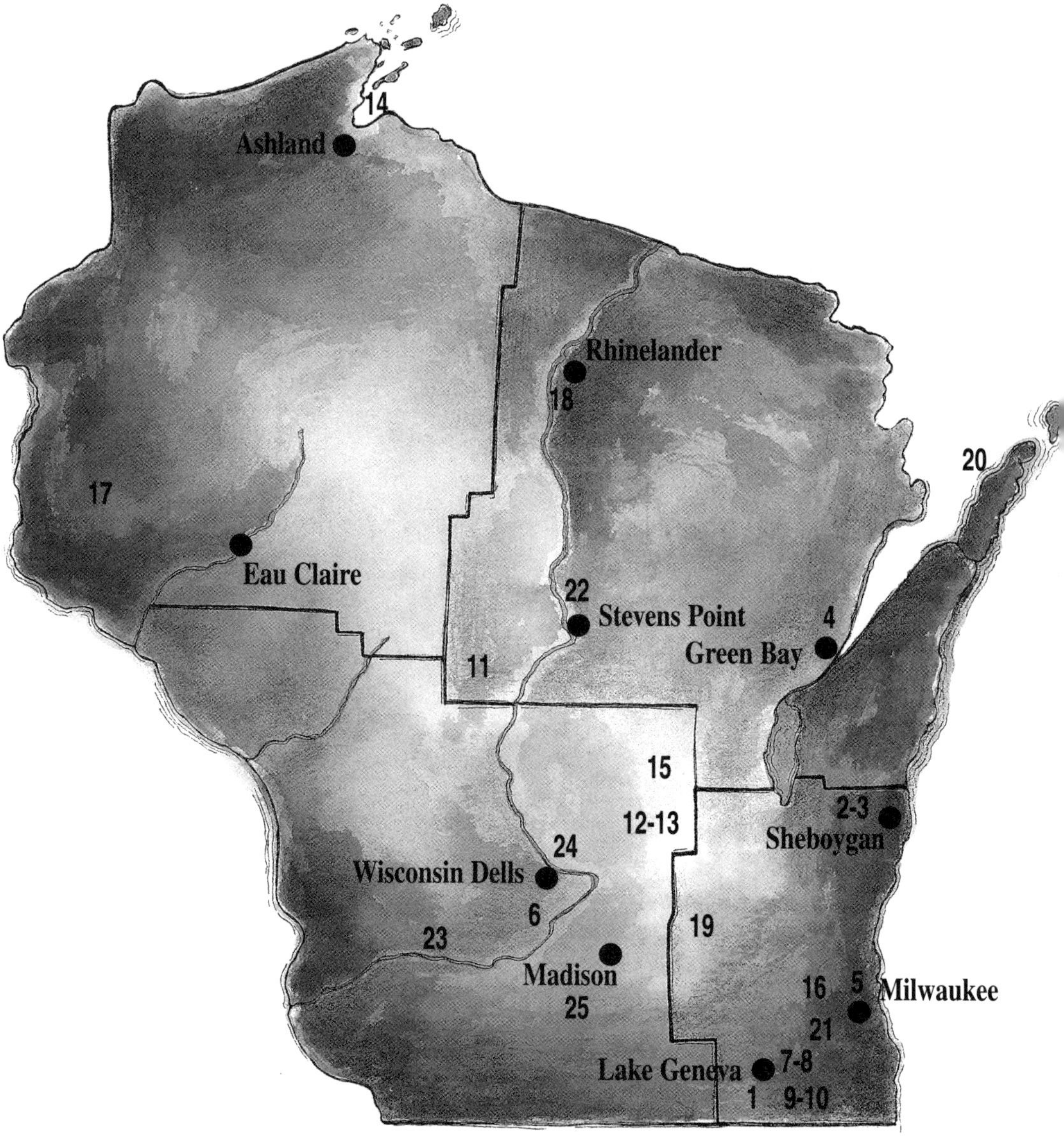

- Ashland 14
- Rhinelander 18
- 17
- Eau Claire
- 22 Stevens Point
- 11
- 4 Green Bay
- 20
- 15
- 12-13
- 2-3 Sheboygan
- 24
- Wisconsin Dells
- 6
- 23
- 19
- Madison
- 25
- 16  5 Milwaukee
- 21
- Lake Geneva  7-8
- 1  9-10

### Fee Codes
$= $15 or less   $$= $15-$25   $$$= $25-$50   $$$$= $50 or more
Based on highest fee for 18 holes

*iv   Great Golf in Wisconsin*

# Table of Contents

Introduction, by John Hughes and Jeff Mayers ............................. iii
ForeWords, by Andy North and Sherri Steinhauer .......................... vi

## 25 of Wisconsin's Best

**1** Abbey Springs, Fontana ................................................................ 1
**2 - 3** Blackwolf Run, Kohler ............................................................ 4
    The River Course and the Meadow Valleys Course
**4** Brown County, Oneida .................................................................. 7
**5** Brown Deer Park, Milwaukee ...................................................... 10
**6** Devil's Head, Merrimac .............................................................. 13
**7 - 8** Geneva National, Lake Geneva ............................................ 16
    The Palmer Course and the Trevino Course
**9 - 10** Grand Geneva Resort & Spa, Lake Geneva ......................... 19
    The Brute and the Briar Patch
**11** Lake Arrowhead, Nekoosa ......................................................... 22
**12 - 13** Lawsonia, Green Lake ........................................................ 25
    The Links Course and the Woodlands Course
**14** Madeline Island ......................................................................... 28
**15** Mascoutin, Berlin ....................................................................... 31
**16** Naga-Waukee, Pewaukee .......................................................... 34
**17** New Richmond ........................................................................... 37
**18** NorthWood, Rhinelander ........................................................... 40
**19** Old Hickory, Beaver Dam ........................................................... 43
**20** Peninsula Park, Fish Creek ........................................................ 46
**21** Rainbow Springs, Mukwonago ................................................... 49
**22** SentryWorld, Stevens Point ....................................................... 52
**23** The Springs, Spring Green ........................................................ 55
**24** Trappers Turn, Wisconsin Dells ................................................. 58
**25** University Ridge, Verona ............................................................ 61

## Plus 311 more

Northwest Courses ......................................................................... 64
Northeast Courses .......................................................................... 84
Southwest Courses ....................................................................... 112
Southeast Courses ....................................................................... 134
Index of Courses .......................................................................... 158

*Great Golf in Wisconsin*

# ForeWords

## By Andy North and Sherri Steinhauer

*Andy North*

We're spoiled, but that's the nature of living in Wisconsin. We're spoiled by a lot of things—including golf—because of the quality of life here.

Wisconsinites, in general, are active, outdoors people no matter the season. We golfers, because our season is so short, are particularly serious about this challenging game. When the snow melts and the grass turns green, we're going to be out there hitting golf balls, and we'll keep at it until the trees are bare in the fall.

What we have here in Wisconsin is a wide variety of courses, ranging from fine older courses, built in the 1920s and earlier, to newer 1980s and 1990s designs—with a lot in between.

There is variety from region to region, too. Golf courses in the northern part of the state are totally different from those in any other part of the state. We've got summer resorts, lots of nine-holers and a great selection of really special 18-hole golf courses with that extraordinary atmosphere—pines, sparkling lakes and marvelous fresh clean air. The quality of golf is enjoyable, the scenery fantastic. There are still places a family can join for $300 to $400 for the summer, where you can turn the kids loose and have a nice golfing experience.

Then you have the major portion of the state—from Stevens Point and Wausau over to the Fox Valley, down to Madison and Milwaukee, where you have a more metropolitan kind of golf. Here you'll find the vast majority of the state's golf courses—some really nice country clubs, but also many great public facilities.

That's what's so nice about golf in Wisconsin. If you can only afford to pay $5 to play golf, you can find places to play. If your budget allows you to pay $25 a round, you can find places for that. And if you don't have to worry about budget, you can find places where you can spend as much as you want. It's like being able to shop at Saks Fifth Avenue or Kmart.

Believe me, golf is not like that everywhere. In most parts of the country the low-end option may be so bad that you don't want to play it, and the high-end option might be way overpriced. In Wisconsin you can find a golf course that will fit your needs and your wallet.

When I played junior and amateur golf in the '60s and early '70s, I played a lot of different courses around the country. That's when I began to realize how good we have it in Wisconsin. We take it for granted that we're going to have bentgrass fairways and bentgrass greens and good tees. That, too, is not the case in a lot of other places. Even some of the courses I played on tour 20 years ago were unbelievably bad. I finished second in Houston one year on greens that didn't have a bit of grass on them; they were just dirt.

And, of course, there are always new courses being built in Wisconsin, and it's encouraging to see that many of them are really first-class public facilities. For many years everybody wanted to build country clubs, but in the last five to 10 years, course developers have said, "Why not bring the same quality to the public golfer?" You may have to pay a little more, but even our expensive public courses here are fairly inexpensive compared to courses in other parts of the country.

I think it comes down to quality and value again. If you can give somebody something that's special and they have a great experience, even if you charge a little bit more for it, it's still a bargain in Wisconsin.

Of all the recreational activities you can be involved in, golf is absolutely the best. It's something you can do your entire life, with your kids, grandkids, grandparents, whomever. If you like to walk, golf is a very nice way to exercise. It's a chance to get out in nature and really enjoy a great game.

For my money, there isn't a better place to play golf than right here in Wisconsin. □

---

*Andy North is a professional golfer and golf course designer from Madison, Wisconsin. He is a two-time winner of the U.S. Open and, along with partner Roger Packard, has designed courses in Wisconsin, Illinois, Colorado and Spain.*

Growing up in Madison, I always enjoyed playing courses in Wisconsin and the Midwest. Sometimes in the summer, when Nakoma Golf Club was too crowded, my dad and mom and I would get in the car and drive over to play at Mount Horeb or Spring Green or at other local courses. You never had to drive far to find a nice, playable golf course.

*Sherri Steinhauer*

The courses in Wisconsin are extremely plush due to the definition of the bentgrass between the fairways and rough, and between the greens and the fringes. Because this is Wisconsin, you have the added beauty of many varieties of trees. The fullness of the maples, oaks and pines in midsummer makes courses even more picturesque.

When I take some time off the tour and get back home, I'm amazed at some of the changes that have taken place. There are great new courses opening all the time. Recently, some of the designers have produced a wide variety, such as University Ridge near Madison, which has one heavily wooded nine and one open, links-type nine. The latest golf course designs are the perfect complement to the older, traditional courses built in the '20s.

It used to be that most of the great courses in the state were private, but that's certainly not the case anymore. Public courses like Blackwolf Run, Lawsonia, The Springs, SentryWorld, University Ridge—and a lot of others—are as good as you'll find anywhere.

People who don't know me very well are always surprised that I come from Wisconsin. They wonder how someone from Wisconsin ever learned to play golf. I usually laugh and tell them there is no place more beautiful than Wisconsin in the summer.

We can't play year round, but in a lot of ways I think that

We can't play year round, but in a lot of ways I think that helped make me a better player. As a youngster I took full advantage of the time I had by playing every day—sometimes as many as 45 or 54 holes. Possibly if I had lived in a warmer climate my interests would have been more diversified and I would have spent less time playing golf.

It's also nice to have a change of seasons. I remember after a long winter, especially once the pro tournaments started on TV in January, I couldn't wait to get out on the course. So spring was always a time to look forward to. It's wonderful to see the flowers bloom and to watch the approach of the warm days of summer, which are really ideal for playing golf. Then the fall is a beautiful time to travel the country roads to various courses and witness the leaves changing color. Because of the change of seasons and the variety of weather conditions they bring, you have the opportunity to build a well-rounded game.

I've had the chance to play golf all over the world, and that's made me truly appreciate the golf courses in Wisconsin—not only because of their beauty but also because they can be played at a reasonable cost.

Add that to the condition of the courses and the terrain, with rolling hills, trees and water—the things I like best about Wisconsin courses—and you can understand why I like to come home. □

*Sherri Steinhauer, another Madison native, has become one of the most consistent players on the LPGA Tour. She earned her first LPGA victory in 1992 and in 1993 passed the $1 million mark in career earnings. Her second tour victory came in 1994.*

# Abbey Springs

*Beyond a doubt, Abbey Springs is one of the prettiest golf courses in southern Wisconsin.*

Driving along Fontana's tree-canopied South Shore Drive, with Geneva Lake glimmering behind the handsome lakeshore homes, you're immediately taken by the beauty of the area. So by the time you turn into the entrance to Abbey Springs Golf Course, you're expecting something special.

You won't be disappointed.

Beyond a doubt, Abbey Springs is one of the prettiest courses in southern Wisconsin. Nature contributed the woods and hills to the setting. The rest is the work of the private resort's staff and an owners association that obviously takes pride in its golf course. The tees, fairways, greens—even the sand traps—are meticulously groomed. Flower gardens, rock-lined streams and areas of rough that have been left rough—marshland, mostly—add to the overall beauty of the layout.

In fall, it's a special treat to stand above treetop level on the 12th or 17th tee and gaze over the green fairways to brilliantly colored woods and Geneva Lake shimmering in the background. The view alone is worth the greens fee.

But there's more to Abbey Springs than beautiful scenery. The par-72 layout measures 6,466 yards from the championship tees. Many holes, however, play much longer or much shorter than the posted yardage because of the terrain.

The 10th hole, for example, is a backbreaking 545 yards from the championship tee and uphill all the way. Trees and underbrush line both sides of the fairway, and the elevated green is pitched from back to front.

Conversely, Nos. 12 and 17, the lake-view holes, play considerably shorter than their respective measured distances of 347 and 320 yards. Both holes seem to invite an attempt to drive the green. This is not a smart play in either case.

A fairway wood—an iron, more likely—hit down the right side of No. 12 will kick the ball toward the middle off the banked fairway, leaving a short iron shot to the green. The situation is similar on No. 17—an iron off the tee, followed by a short approach shot.

If something inside says you simply have to attempt to drive the green, be aware that both greens are small and well-protected. Sand traps to the left and right of the 12th green leave only a narrow opening to the putting surface, which slopes slightly from front to back. The 17th green has a steep-faced bunker at the front, with a marshy hazard to the left and rear. Don't say you weren't warned.

The 13th hole measures 315 yards but plays longer because it's all uphill. It also features a two-tiered green with as much elevation difference between the tiers as you're likely to encounter on any course.

Want more?

The 14th hole is a 520-yard par 5 that offers a blind tee shot to a narrow fairway. But take heart. Mounding along both sides of the fairway helps keep the ball in play.

The second shot will be a lay-up short of a pond that has a narrow strip of beach along its front edge. The approach is to a shallow green with a significant back-to-front slope.

Perhaps the most difficult hole at Abbey Springs is the par-4 15th, which measures 467 yards from the championship tee. (You get a meager 12-yard advantage by moving up to the white tee.) The drive is into the upslope of the fairway, which reduces roll to almost nothing and leaves you with a second shot of from 200 to 260 yards, depending on your strength off the tee. There's also a large sand trap in front of the green—something to consider as you line up that long approach shot.

Designed by Ken Killian and Dick Nugent, Abbey Springs opened in 1972. Since the Lake Geneva area had long been a popular playground for the wealthy from the Chicago area, it seemed a sure bet that a golf course such as Abbey Springs would succeed, if only for the easy access it offered the Illinois crowd.

But despite its beautiful location, Abbey Springs struggled through the mid- and late-1970s. In 1981, the course was sold to a group of home owners who held possession of the property surrounding it.

Taking a direction that emphasized improvement of the course, the new owners, some 500 in all, hired Dave Smith as course superintendent. Smith, who was schooled in California, had worked for three years at the famed Pebble Beach Golf Links.

Under his direction, small tees and greens were rebuilt and enlarged, bunkers were added, the irrigation system was upgraded, and drainage was improved. Slowly but steadily, the course took on the shape the designers originally envisioned.

Jack Shoger, the head professional at Abbey Springs since 1984, has watched the transformation take place. One of the first steps taken was to improve the condition of the fairways. "We've followed a serious program of top-dressing, overseeding, aeration and fertilization for a number of years," he said. Reseeding the fairways with bentgrass has given the course the look and playability of a country club layout.

All changes have been made with the original design in mind. While Killian and Nugent are no longer together, the firm of Killian and Associates oversees the improvements.

"We're committed to going with their master plan," Shoger said. "And we're getting pretty darned close now. It's come a long way since my first days."

Things have also come a long way for the owners, and the land around their much-improved golf course is sold out.

Since Abbey Springs is a weekend retreat for most of its owners, the public is welcome to help fill out tee times. Only the golf course, bar and banquet facilities at the complex are open to the public. Other amenities at Abbey Springs, including the yacht club, marina and a restaurant adjacent to the golf course, are open to members only. □

 **ABBEY SPRINGS GOLF COURSE**
South Shore Drive • Fontana 53125 • 414/275-6113

**Directions:** 1 1/2 miles east of Hwy. 67 on South Shore Drive (Fontana Boulevard)
**Course:** 18 holes/par 72/6,466 yards
**Fee:** $$$$    Carts required (Fee includes cart)

# Blackwolf Run

*Every practice stroke, every shot, every thought demands complete attention.*

So you want to play a golf course where your high score can be worn as a badge of honor?

Welcome to Blackwolf Run, a 36-hole golf complex that's sure to raise your handicap, steal your golf balls, and lighten your wallet while, at the same time, making you happy to be alive and playing this crazy game.

Thank designer Pete Dye and bathroom fixtures king Herb Kohler Jr. for that tingling feeling you get when lofting a career drive over the 100-foot-high large-toothed aspens on the 337-yard par-4 "Cathedral Spires" hole on the River Course. Curse them when you pull your robust approach shot into the Sheboygan River on the demanding, 560-yard par-5 16th hole, "Unter Der Linden."

Such are the ups and downs, twists and turns your golf ball will take on the River and Meadow Valleys courses at Kohler's golf kingdom. It's a kingdom carved from his vast nature preserve, River Wildlife, along the Sheboygan River in east-central Wisconsin, near Lake Michigan. It's a kingdom once claimed by the Winnebago Indians, who in the early 19th century had a chief named Black Wolf. It's a kingdom that will gain even more national exposure when the U.S. Women's Open Championship will be staged here in 1998.

Here—in a place where salmon make their fall spawning runs, where herons swoop into secretive hiding spots, and deer peek from wood's edge—two strong-willed golf nuts created something that a lot of other golf nuts think is worth up to $91 per round. It's more than the fact that these are two of the best golf courses in the Midwest.

"You can't find one spot on this golf course that you won't enjoy, just standing and looking," Dye said at Blackwolf Run's opening in 1988. "You might be playing like hell. You might have lost seven golf balls. But if you just stop and look around, you'll come back tomorrow, because the scenery—the whole atmosphere—is just tremendous."

But it's playing the courses that sticks with you most. Every practice stroke, every shot, every thought demands complete attention. Slack off here, and you'll pay for it in strokes. The slope ratings tell the tale: 151

(a slope rating of more than 130 is considered difficult) on the wooded, water-bound River Course; 143 on the open but longer and windswept Valleys layout, which is appreciably different and much kinder from the forward tees.

Tough? You bet. During an exhibition stop in 1990, touring pro Paul Azinger managed no better than a 76 on the River Course.

That's just what Dye's audience wants.

"The prime objective I have in building a golf course is that I want to attract the guy with the 19 handicap who loves the game of golf," Dye says. "They're going to lose golf balls. They're going to be in ditches...I don't quite understand why they keep coming back, but they will."

And they have, despite green fees that are steep by Wisconsin standards. They're drawn by the reviews, by the beautiful natural setting and by the luxurious accommodations available at The American Club, Kohler's five-diamond-award resort. Blackwolf Run has become a stop for the international traveling golfer.

The two courses are very different—testimony to the area's varying terrain, Dye's dastardly designing mind and Kohler's millions.

The showcase River Course makes use of the dark, twisty Sheboygan River and its steep banks, which sweep into play on 14 of 18 holes. Thick woods fill out the scenery.

The links-style Meadow Valleys Course lies primarily on grassy uplands. Pockets of trees, drastic pitches and draws, and massive sand traps characterize this masterpiece. You know the sand traps are big when you must use steps to walk into them.

The signature hole on the 18 is No. 15, "Mercy," which golfers are heard to cry when their shots go awry. The mesalike green on the 227-yard par 3 falls off steeply in nearly every direction. Between the tee and the 53-yard-long green, you'll encounter a gorge filled with wiry vegetation. Mercy!

In all, the two courses cover 400 acres of prime Wisconsin real estate—minus some of the original trees but including two greens on Valleys' 18th hole. (The green short of the Sheboygan River is for those playing the red tees.) The trees didn't go without a fight. Kohler hated to see each one go.

"Pete and I have spent many hours walking this ground," said Kohler, an avid golfer with a handicap in the double digits. "We've had our battles."

"It's not wide open, but it's a helluva lot better than it was," joked Dye. One oft-told story had Dye using some trickery to get his way on the old par-3 eighth on the River Course.

"The way I wanted it gave you a nice river walk through the

woods from green to [the next] tee. Pete has a real problem with long green-to-tee walks," Kohler recalled to interviewers.

Kohler's idea had the green snuggling up to the river. Dye wanted the green closer to the next tee, which meant downing some trees. The tug of war went on for more than a year and a half. Finally, a meeting was arranged to resolve the dispute.

But pressing company business kept Kohler from making his 5 p.m. appointment. When Kohler finally arrived, Dye was gone.

"I didn't think much of it," Kohler said. "He'd be back in a couple of weeks, and we could look at it then."

Not quite. The next morning Kohler discovered he'd been fooled.

"That son of a gun had...at five o'clock called all of the crew together, and he'd said, 'I want that area down there cleaned out in one hour, and in one more hour I want the green built.' In about an hour and three-quarters he not only had the whole area cleared, but he had mounds of earth moved in and the green was shaped.

"That was brute force in action," Kohler said.

Even Kohler concedes that Dye's brute force made for a better golf course. But it was Kohler's vision that made Blackwolf Run happen.

When the Kohler Company decided to go into the resort business, the locals called it "Kohler's Folly." But the joke's on those who don't play Blackwolf Run. □

## BLACKWOLF RUN
1111 W. Riverside Drive • Kohler 53044 • 414/457-4446

**Directions:** I-94 west to Milwaukee, then I-43 north to exit 126, west onto Hwy. 23, exit Co. Y (Kohler), south into Kohler
**Course:** River Course, 18 holes/par72/6,991 yards;
  Meadow Valleys Course, 18 holes/par 72/7,142 yards
**Fee:** $$$$   Tee times required
**Amenities:** Pro shop; restaurant; bar; driving range;
  locker room; meeting & banquet facilities; lesson program

# Brown County

*A magnificent course in the traditional sense.*

When Wisconsin football fans see autumn's green and gold, they think Green Bay Packers football. But golfers should think of playing "The County," a dandy municipal course in Green Bay's back yard, not far from Lombardi Avenue and Lambeau Field.

At Brown County Golf Course in nearby Oneida, golden leaves and green, tree-lined fairways provide a lovely setting for one of the last rounds of the year. A colorful October day may be enhanced by noisy flights of Canada geese traveling south to warmer winter climes.

Once, good timing could provide a leisurely round of golf at this time of year. But the exploding popularity of the game and the discovery of "The County" (it's hard to keep a good secret when a course keeps appearing on *Golf Digest* magazine's "best" lists) have made that difficult to accomplish in recent years.

No matter. It's worth the time it takes to play even a long round at Brown County.

Such opportunities didn't always exist in the Green Bay area. Back in 1948, things looked grim for public course golfers. The 18-hole public course in town was on the verge of going private, which would have left a marginal nine-hole track and a private 18-hole layout (Oneida Golf & Riding Club).

Enter a group of dedicated golfers led by Bob Barclay, an ordinary citizen and self-described "golf nut."

"I guess I fell into it because I felt so strongly about it," Barclay said.

Barclay circulated petitions backing an 18-hole public course and took them to the city. City officials turned him down but suggested he try the county government. He did, and with the help of friendly coverage from the local newspaper's sports editor and some key officials and civic leaders, eventually convinced the county board that building a golf course would be a good idea. Barclay and his supporters even forced a change in state law, which prohibited any county other than Milwaukee County from building a golf course.

The Brown County board approved the project on Sept. 1, 1955, appointing Barclay to the committee assigned to bring the project to reality. Three years and some $670,000 later, Brown County had a new golf course. The course officially opened on Aug. 4, 1958. "I hit the first ball on it," said Barclay, calling his lobbying effort an "adventure."

In these days of government boondoggles, the Brown County Golf Course was a real success story. Not only did the county purchase a fine piece of real estate, it hired Lawrence Packard, a fine golf course architect, to design it.

"We were just getting started," Packard recalled. "It was one of our first 18-hole, regulation, big-time jobs."

Packard didn't use many gimmicks in designing the par-72 layout that measures 6,729 yards from the back tees, nor did he have to. The natural material for a masterpiece was already in place: rolling, glaciated terrain characterized by healthy stands of mature hardwoods and ample flowing waters in the form of Duck and Trout creeks. Duck Creek and its tributary can come into play on eight of the course's 18 holes.

"We knew we had an excellent site," Barclay said. "The architect really convinced us it had everything. The course has proved it's true."

One key stretch of the course along Duck Creek has been described as Brown County's version of Augusta National's "Amen Corner." The three-hole test begins at No. 11, a 442-yard par 4. From the tee, which has a wonderful view of the countryside, a dogleg runs downhill to the right, with heavy woods along the right side—definitely the side to avoid.

The 12th hole is a tricky, 399-yard par 4 that presents big problems to the spray hitter. Duck Creek and the gnarled trees that line the skinny fairway can turn a pleasant outing into disaster. Use something other than a driver off the tee, aiming for the wide part of the fairway where it takes a slight turn to the right.

At 349 yards, No. 13 is shorter but no less challenging, thanks to more trees and water. Getting to the severe dogleg of this right-to-left hole is only the first step. You'll then have to cope with three ponds that make the target look like an island green. Sand also guards the severely sloping green, just in case the water hasn't made you nervous enough. If you manage bogey or better, say "Amen."

In addition to making good use of the creeks, Packard mixed in some 50 sand traps (four fairway traps have recently been added on Nos. 1, 8 and 16) and varied the length and size of the greens.

Highly regarded from the outset, the course began receiving national attention after a move designed to reduce maintenance costs also enhanced Packard's design, according to Roger Vander

Leest, a county board member with a deep interest in the course. Instead of cutting fairways from tree line to tree line, course managers decided to leave more areas unmowed. Maintenance costs were reduced by one-third, and the bentgrass fairways were narrowed, said Vander Leest, noting that the strategy improved the character of the golf course. Several championship tees have also been added in recent years. The trite, but accurate, thing to say is that good golfers need to use every club in the bag.

In 1959, Packard recalled, some of Wisconsin's best golfers, competing in the State Open Championship at Brown County, complained that the course was too tough. Bobby Brue, now of the professional Senior Tour (then pro at North Hills Country Club), put that to rest by shooting a sizzling 64 that helped clinch a victory for him—and Packard.

"He kind of bailed us out," Packard said.

While there are now other public courses in the Green Bay area, Brown County is certainly the best. "It just kind of happened," said Vander Leest. "I don't think the county set out to have one of the best [public] courses in the country."

But that's what it is. "A tremendous asset," Vander Leest said. "It brings a lot of people into Brown County."

Even in autumn, when, for golfers, an outing at "The County" can have more allure than the football Packers. □

## BROWN COUNTY GOLF COURSE
897 Riverdale • Oneida 54155 • 414/497-1731

**Directions:** West of Green Bay on Co. J
**Course:** 18 holes/par 72/6,729 yards
**Fee:** $$

# Brown Deer Park

*Brown Deer Park may eventually be ranked as one of the top five public courses in the country.*

Brown Deer Park Golf Course was once a shining example of public golf at its finest.

Built in the late 1920s on farmland that was part of a spacious, wooded park north of Milwaukee, Brown Deer is one of five county courses designed by George Hansen, a longtime county parks superintendent. It's the centerpiece of the 16 courses in the Milwaukee County park system.

Brown Deer Park hosted the United States Golf Association Public Links Championship in 1951, 1966 and 1977, and was ranked among the top 10 public golf courses in the country by *Golf Digest* magazine—right up there with Cog Hill in Illinois and Torrey Pines in California.

Oh, how far and how fast it tumbled.

By the mid-1980s the course was suffering from severe drainage problems, weedy fairways, spotty greens, dying trees and dilapidated bridges—conditions brought on mainly by deterioration of the original clay drainage tiles and a recession-strapped government.

But Brown Deer Park is on the way back. It's a transformation being pushed by the coming of the PGA Tour's Greater Milwaukee Open, which moves to Brown Deer beginning with the 1994 event.

County officials acknowledged they were close to losing their tarnished jewel for good and in the late 1980s decided to invest in its future. The drainage and irrigation systems were replaced and new bridges were built. By late 1989, the course had a new pond, located between the 11th green and the 10th fairway, which improved both holes and provided a boost to the drainage and irrigation systems. The sprawling, undulating greens and big, deep bunkers that characterize the course were restored, and fairways were reseeded with bentgrass.

The Greater Milwaukee Open's announcement that it would move the tournament from Tuckaway Country Club in Franklin, where it had been held for 21 years, to Brown Deer Park all but ensured a return to national prominence for the venerable public layout.

The GMO, in partnership with the Wisconsin PGA, which

manages the golf operation at Brown Deer Park, earmarked $900,000 for immediate improvements to bring the course up to PGA Tour standards. The partnership, called Greater Milwaukee Golf Management Inc., hired the design team of Roger Packard and Andy North to make the necessary changes.

North, the two-time U.S. Open champion from Madison, and Packard, who's been involved in the design or renovation of more than a dozen Wisconsin courses, sought early input from tour professionals, including 1992 GMO winner Richard Zokol, 1990 winner Jim Gallagher Jr., Jeff Sluman and Billy Andrade. To a man, the pros concluded that Brown Deer was a classic course that needed little beyond cosmetic changes.

Perhaps the most significant change that North and Packard made was to the 18th hole, previously a monster of 576 yards. They moved the green closer to the tee by about 40 yards, which alleviated congestion near the clubhouse—an important consideration during the GMO, which draws more than 25,000 fans daily. The move also made the green reachable in two shots, although the hole does not necessarily play easier. Added traps and green contouring increase the risk-and-reward factor for those who try to reach the green in two.

North and Packard also redesigned the fifth hole, one of three par 3s on the front nine. The new tee is now to the left of the old tee area, and a new green was built in an opening among the trees behind the old green. The tee on No. 8, a 440-yard par 4, was elevated and moved back, and greens on Nos. 9, 10 and 14 were rebuilt. In addition, bunkers were added on Nos. 15, 16, 17 and 18.

Other changes included construction of a state-of-the-art bentgrass practice area, with greens for chipping and putting, and two practice sand traps. The 60-year-old clubhouse received a face-lift that included remodeled locker rooms to replace facilities that had begun to resemble something from a medieval castle.

But even with the changes, it's significant to note how much of the course has not changed. In essence, George Hansen's design has stood the test of time.

Hansen was a young golf pro at Racine's public course when the Milwaukee County Park Commission hired him in 1919 to lay out the county's first course, Grant Park, overlooking Lake Michigan in South Milwaukee. Appointed parks superintendent in 1926, Hansen followed through with four other 18-hole county courses—Greenfield in West Allis, Currie in Wauwatosa, Whitnall in Hales Corners and Brown Deer.

While Hansen's courses are all solid tests of golf, Brown Deer Park has long been recognized as the best of the lot.

The setting is decidedly parklike—a vast expanse of grass, with gentle hills and tall, mature trees. Since it's a busy public course, it's important to keep play moving. The roughs, therefore, are cut low, and while trees abound, shots that land among them are generally recoverable.

Much of the course's challenge lies in its length—six par 4s that are 413 yards or longer from the championship tees, a par 3 of 215 yards (No. 7), two more that are a shade under 200 yards and a couple of genuine three-shot par 5s.

The second hole is a good example of the difficult par 4s–421 yards long, with an uphill second shot to a severely sloping green.

The fourth hole, formerly a short par 5, is now a 486-yard par 4. For those of us not playing in the GMO, it's still going to be a par 5, for all practical purposes. The waterway that cuts through eight fairways on the course crosses the fourth fairway about 125 to 150 yards in front of the green, adding suspense to the decision of whether to go for broke or lay up on the second shot.

No. 10 is a par 4 that stretches to 459 yards, with a slight bend to the right. The pond, added during the 1980s restoration, hugs the corner on the left. The long second shot is uphill to a narrow green guarded by trees and sand traps.

The 18th hole, though shortened, remains a classic test of golf. The waterway cuts through at about 180 yards—at the front edge. It takes a shot of 210 to 215 yards to carry the water, and that's something for even the reasonably long hitter to think about.

More changes will be made at Brown Deer Park over the next several years. Eventually, all of the greens will be rebuilt. Other, more subtle refinements will be made as necessary. The end result, bragged Andy North, will be a course that will rank among the top five public facilities in the country.

The best part is that both hackers and pros will be able to enjoy Brown Deer's comeback. □

## BROWN DEER GOLF COURSE
7835 N. Brown Deer Road • Milwaukee 53209 • 414/352-8080

**Directions:** Exit I-43, west on Good Hope to Range Line Road, then follow signs
**Course:** 18 holes/par 71/6,763 yards
**Fee:** $$$

# Devil's Head

*Set amid the ancient, rock-strewn Baraboo Hills, Devil's Head is a heavenly trip for the touring golfer.*

You know you're in for something different when the starter hands you a lift ticket in lieu of a bag tag at the beginning of your round.

Welcome to Devil's Head Resort and Convention Center—a ski resort in winter, a golf resort for most of the rest of the year.

Set amid the ancient, rock-strewn Baraboo Hills, Devil's Head is a heavenly trip for the touring golfer, with pretty vistas, pleasant breezes, trees galore and a variety of wildlife. Hawks riding the thermals above the ski runs are a common sight. Songbirds frequent feeders strategically located along the fairways. In spring, apple blossoms add a fragrant, colorful touch to the scene.

Oh, yes, there's a terrific golf course, too.

Thank Willis Stoick and Art Johnson for that. Stoick is a Michigan developer who also had a hand in developing Alpine Valley, near East Troy. Johnson, of Madison, designed two of the capital city's major municipal courses, Odana Hills and Yahara Hills.

Devil's Head was born in 1971. The golf course, lodge and ski trails were all completed in one year.

"Willis wore two hats," Johnson recalled. "He was the boss, and he drove the graders and the earth movers. The golf course was an important part of the resort to him."

They didn't have to move much dirt to craft the layout, which gives you the feeling of playing a course in the Appalachians or foothills of the Rockies. Even if they had been tempted to outdo the glacier's work, a layer of granite close to the surface kept them in line.

"The area was beautiful," Johnson said. "We were able to conserve the natural amenities. We used the rolling topography and existing woods."

That's evident everywhere—from the nifty, tree-saturated, par-4 second hole to the breathtaking contrast between tee and fairway on the par-5 fourth hole. Add some water—or a lot of it, in the case of Nos. 5 and 6—and you've got a course that captures the feel of this uncharacteristically rugged Midwest landscape.

*Great Golf in Wisconsin* 13

Stoick and Johnson even found use for an old stone wall that cuts prominently across the 13th and 14th fairways. The three-foot-high wall provides a unique hazard and a reminder that even a bad day of golf beats trying to farm this land. "The farmer really put a lot of backbreaking work into it, so we left it there," Johnson said.

Chances are, you won't see many golf course signs like two here that show the wear of hard weather and flying golf balls: "Beware of ricochet," "If ball within 10 yards of wall, free drop."

Hopefully you'll avoid that occurrence. But THE WALL is definitely an intimidating factor, especially on No. 13, which measures 447 yards from the back tees—as if a 447-yard par 4 isn't intimidating enough.

This hole is in a run of four (Nos. 12 through 15) that gives you the sense of cruising through alpine meadows. The tee box is elevated—not as high as the top of the ski hill but high enough to allow you to see what you're getting into.

The wall is down there aways, flanked on both sides by trees. Even though it's downhill, you'll need to hit a driver so you can reach the green in two. Aim slightly toward a group of small pines on the left and let the slope of the fairway put you into position. From there, a lofted wood from the downhill lie will probably reach the elevated green. If that shot goes up and over and reasonably straight, the worst you'll likely end up with is a wedge shot to the green. There's even a hole in the stone wall big enough to drive a cart through. Consider par a very good score here.

The uphill, par-5 14th, which comes back the other way, isn't nearly as difficult because it opens up considerably after the drive. The wall here is fairly close to the tee, so only a poor tee shot will be in danger of the dreaded ricochet.

On the 15th hole, a devilishly difficult par 4, remnants of the wall lie in a thin line of leafy trees on the right, inside the elbow of a downhill dogleg. There's an opening in the wall for those who choose the more direct, and easier, trek to the hole.

The checkered marker flag is atop a ridge with a landing area that's too small. Put the driver away and hit a little short and right to the broad flats. Then loft a short iron to the small green backed by cedars and sumac bushes.

Next it's down into the valley for a trio of solid finishing holes. Number 16 is a sweeping, rather open, downhill par 5, where a big hitter can think eagle with the correct hooking drive around the big tree on the left side. The 17th hole is a tricky par 3 that calls for a straight shot through trees that stand on either side of the entryway to the elevated green.

Finally, there's the intimidator, No. 18, which may make the holes featuring the wall seem tame by comparison. This 424-yard par 4 is one tough finishing hole. From the elevated tee, drive to the open right side. Then it's a long iron shot over water to a green backed by a bunker and a hill. The shot is all carry. Bail out to the right side if you have any doubts.

After it all, put your clubs away and relax at the 250-room resort, which features dining, swimming and exercise facilities. There are also hiking and biking trails and tennis courts. If you stay long enough, you may even get to try the ski slopes. Wisconsin summers in the Baraboo Hills are short but very, very sweet. □

## DEVIL'S HEAD LODGE
S6330 Bluff Road • Merrimac 53561 • 608/493-2251

**Directions:** Thirty miles north of Madison on I-90/94, exit 108 on Hwy. 78 for eight miles, right on Co. DL to Bluff Road
**Course:** 18 holes/par 73/6,725 yards
**Fee:** $$$    Tee times required; carts required until 4 p.m.

# Geneva National

*Arnold Palmer and Lee Trevino, two of the greatest players in the history of the game, have designed two of Wisconsin's finest courses.*

The Palmer Course and the Trevino Course

Bring Arnold Palmer and Lee Trevino on board to design your golf courses and you'll get one benefit above all others: You'll get Arnold Palmer and Lee Trevino. They'll be there for the initial press conference, for occasional visits during construction and for the all-important grand opening. At that time they'll play golf, chat amiably with the fans, and schmooze into the evening with well-wishers in a grand reception hall.

So it was at Geneva National Golf Club. On a sunny August day in 1991, Lee Trevino christened the course that bears his name by shooting a 6-under-par 66. The next day Arnold Palmer played an exhibition on his course and shot an even-par 72. "I heard what he shot on his course, and that must be a lot easier than mine," Palmer quipped.

Actually, the two courses have about the same level of difficulty. The Palmer Course is 7,171 yards from the championship tees; the Trevino Course is 7,120. Both courses have five sets of tee boxes on each hole, which is how the two designers/legends made their courses challenging for the very best players, yet manageable for the rest of us. Having the names of Palmer and Trevino attached to its golf courses is important to the Illinois-based Anvan Development Company, which produced the 1,600-acre residential-recreational Geneva National community along the shores of Lake Como in the heart of the Lake Geneva vacation area. The status of a link with Palmer and Trevino helps sell the condominiums and homesites.

Having Palmer and Trevino involved also ensures the quality of the golf courses. Palmer's design company, especially, is recognized worldwide for its work.

The glacier-carved terrain of both courses at Geneva National is similar: rolling, almost to the point of being hilly, and heavily wooded with maple, oak, walnut and hickory. Off the manicured bentgrass fairways and away from the houses and condos, the land is virtually undisturbed. There are streams and ponds and marshy wetlands inhabited by ducks and geese. Often a shot must carry a ravine overgrown with brush and wildflowers.

"When you play the course, you will have thought it was here for fifty years," Trevino said of his layout.

The Trevino Course begins and ends in heavy forest. In between are several open holes, some of which are bordered by wetlands. Most tees are elevated because, as Trevino said, "I don't know of a soul who doesn't like to stand up on the tee and look like he's shooting down at the whole world."

Several greens on the Trevino Course are cut into the side of a hill, which means they're friendly on the high side, where a shot might kick toward the putting surface, and dangerous on the low side, where a stray shot has a chance of bounding down into a steep bunker or off into the trees. On these holes, it's more important to note the slope than the position of the flagstick on the approach shots.

The fifth hole is recognized as the signature hole on the Trevino layout. It's a mirror image of the 13th at Augusta National, home of the Masters. The 13th at Augusta is a short par 5 with a dogleg left. The second shot is a lay-up short of Rae's Creek, or a daring blast over it. At 520 yards from the championship tees, No. 5 on the Trevino Course is a bit longer, and it bends left to right. The challenge on the second shot is the same as at Augusta—the green is potentially reachable in two, but the meandering creek provides a severe penalty if you miss.

The Palmer Course also begins in a heavily wooded area before opening up on the eighth hole, a difficult par 3 of 227 yards from the championship tee (218 from the blue and 195 from the copper). If length weren't enough of a challenge, the green is tucked behind the corner of a pond, making the direct route all carry. Large sand traps discourage bailing out to the left.

Palmer immodestly calls the 393-yard, par-4 15th hole, "just a tremendous golf hole." There's a wide open fairway to the left, which narrows quickly as it reaches a bend to the right that's guarded by a pond. Standing on the elevated tee, "You take off just as much as your guts will let you take off," as Palmer put it, with a gleam in his eye.

Number 16 is another long par 3 (218 yards from the back tee) that backs right up to Lake Como. It's slightly downhill, and the ground behind the green falls away toward the water. From the tee, it looks as if the lake is right against the back edge of the green.

The 17th hole is another Palmer favorite. Like the 18th hole at Pebble Beach, which is bordered on the left by the Pacific Ocean, the 17th on the Palmer Course follows the shoreline of Lake Como. You can see the green from the tee, but it looks awfully far away, with nothing but water between tee and green. Golfers with the desire to get home in two may try a dangerous path along the water's edge. It's shorter, but very risky.

Taking the fairway route has its trials, as well. There's a large landing area for the second shot, but it's easy to drive through the fairway and into sand traps. The green slopes back towards the lake, and from 100 yards away the flagstick looks like it's sticking up from the water. Psychologically, it's a difficult approach shot.

Number 18 heads back toward the massive, three-level clubhouse and has hip-high grass to the left and a handful of sand traps guarding the edges of the squiggly fairway. You'll have to pick your way through the hazards to the green.

Only one of Geneva National's courses is open to the public on a given day, while the other is reserved for members. They alternate daily.

A third course, this one designed by Gary Player, another golfing legend, is under construction at Geneva National, but concerns for preserving wetlands near Lake Como have caused delays. It's hoped the first nine holes will be ready for play by late 1994 or early 1995, with work on the second nine scheduled to begin at that time.

In addition to golf, the Geneva National community has a hunt club, a racquet and swim club, tennis courts and a sporting clays course. The area is zoned for 1,900 residential units, many of which were sold the first year. These are mainly second homes for the residents, the majority of whom are from the Chicago area.

It's said that some of the residents don't even play golf. That's their loss because two of the greatest players in the history of the game have created some fine courses right in their back yards. □

### GENEVA NATIONAL GOLF CLUB
1221 Geneva National Avenue South • Lake Geneva 53147 • 414/245-7010

**Directions:** Four miles west of Lake Geneva on Hwy. 50, or one-half mile east of intersection of Hwys. 50 and 67
**Course:** Palmer Course, 18 holes/par 72/7,171 yards; Trevino Course, 18 holes/par 72/7,120 yards
**Fee:** $$$$    Tee times and carts required
**Amenities:** Pro shop; driving range; lessons; golf school; locker room; club storage; valet parking; banquet facilities

# Grand Geneva Resort & Spa

*The Brute and the Briar Patch were unlike any courses Wisconsin had ever seen–layouts as showy as the performers who worked its nightclubs.*

### The Brute and the Briar Patch

Bob Hope performed here. So did Henny Youngman and Richard Pryor. Cher tried the putting green while wearing spike heels. Tony Randall and Sammy Davis Jr. were on hand for the grand opening.

Many Hollywood and Las Vegas stars appeared at the Lake Geneva Playboy Club in the 1960s and '70s. The hip nightclubs, featuring big-name entertainers and a bevy of beautiful bunnies, were in their prime in big cities across the nation, so this was real glitz for Wisconsin. At Lake Geneva, a traditional playground for the wealthy of northern Illinois and southern Wisconsin, it was something different—a full-scale resort, with both hedonistic and athletic diversions, including two terrific golf courses named the Brute and the Briar Patch.

The Playboy bunnies are long gone, although reminders of their presence—such as the "bunny dormitories" along the left side of the Brute's No. 2 fairway—remain.

Now owned by the Marcus Corporation, the 357-room resort has been given a multimillion-dollar overhaul and renamed the Grand Geneva Resort & Spa. And the golf courses have been returned to a level of quality after a period of inattentive maintenance.

At the time they were built, the Brute and the Briar Patch were unlike any courses Wisconsin had ever seen—layouts as showy as the performers who worked at the nightclub.

The Brute came first. Designed by an elderly Robert Bruce Harris (who also designed Janesville's Riverside Golf Course), it was completed in 1968 at a cost of about $1.8 million—expensive for the time. It's a long, spacious par-72 layout, 6,997 yards from the championship tees and marked by elevated tees and greens, 68 sand traps and water that comes into play on nine holes. Some of the sand traps are huge, dwarfed only by the massive greens.

The Brute, especially on a breezy day, still lives up to its name. It's no surprise, then, that a concrete sculpture near No. 16, a leftover from the Playboy days, is described as an abstract representation of a frustrated golfer on his knees.

If No. 16, a tough, 190-yard par 3 surrounded on three sides by sand, doesn't bring you to your knees, the 17th and 18th holes may.

The 17th hole, measuring 416 yards from the elevated back tees, requires a long, precise tee shot to a landing strip with a big pond on the right and a sand trap on the left. If you manage that, the second shot is just as demanding—a long shot over a stream and sand to the putting surface.

The 18th hole is a monster—464 yards long, with the old Bunny Lake to the right. The water isn't really a factor until the second shot, when it sneaks into play just before the bowl-shaped green area. The tough holes aren't limited to the back nine. The third hole, a 374-yard par 4, requires great care. The fairway slopes abruptly downhill, where two ponds pinch it to a narrow isthmus 253 yards from the tee. Use an iron off the tee, then try to land another iron shot on the sloping, highly elevated green.

The 421-yard par-4 ninth hole is a backbreaking way to finish the nine-hole round. From an elevated tee, you'll need to hit the ball far enough down the fairway to miss water on the left and right. The second shot, uphill past a big bunker, is tough to gauge.

The Briar Patch, completed in 1971, is very different from the Brute, but no less distinctive. The design was the work of a couple of fellows named Nicklaus and Dye. Jack Nicklaus, then barely into his 30s, was already a golf legend, with three dozen PGA titles to his credit, including six majors. Pete Dye had been designing golf courses for more than a decade, although he was far from reaching the revered status he holds today.

Together, they drew up a quirky little par-71 course that's more than 500 yards shorter than the Brute. But it's a tough little devil, right from the start, with the unmistakable look of a Dye layout. There are narrow (sometimes nearly nonexistent) landing areas, huge traps, elevated tees and elevated greens. Dye made the most of bushy hills and swampy land, and the course has the untamed feel of many of his later designs. It looks more like a Dye course than a Nicklaus course because Nicklaus left halfway through the project after a dispute with the Playboy Club planning committee.

Dye does not look back on the project with a tremendous degree of satisfaction either. He was forced to change the original design several times, he said, to accommodate, among other things, an airstrip.

"That would have been a nice piece of land," Dye said, years later. "Then they decided to put in an airport, a horse farm, a ski hill—all after we started the golf course. So it kind of got screwed up a little bit."

But Dye's work wasn't wasted. You'll find that out early, on successive holes. The third hole is a 326-yard par 4 that's made extremely difficult by three trees in the left half of the fairway at the outer edge of a dogleg. The trees, which begin 275 yards from the tee, could block your approach shot to a very shallow green.

The fourth hole is a par 4 that might well be found in Florida. From a sliver of a tee in a marsh, you'll have to fly the ball more than 200 yards over a creeping stream to a sloping oval green framed by a semicircle of railroad ties and three new traps.

On the back nine, it's a par 5 and a par 4 that demand your attention. The 11th hole, a 562-yard par 5, makes you flirt with a huge, sandy waste area on the second and third shots. The 18th hole, a 390-yard uphill par 4, also has a big, sandy area on the left that will snag many balls from golfers who try to make up for a short drive to the left. The slender green is backed by three narrow, terraced sand traps.

For many years, the fine golf offered here has been overshadowed by memories of the Playboy Club.

Ken Judd was the resort's pro for more than 20 years. "I gave lessons to Christie Hefner (Hugh's daughter) when she was just a little girl," he said. Judd watched not only celebrities come and go but resort management, as well. "We had 15 general managers in 15 years," he said. "One lasted 48 hours."

By the early 1980s, the Playboy Club idea had about run its course. In 1982, Playboy Enterprises Inc. sold the resort to a partnership of Americana Hotels Inc. and a trio of Chicago real estate men, who turned the Bunny Hutch lounge into a disco. The big, man-made body of water called Bunny Lake also lost its name. More ownership changes followed, and both golf courses suffered from neglect.

But that's begun to change in recent years. The 1,300-acre resort-conference center is today a place for families, with well-maintained ski hills, a remodeled health club and spa, and a daycare center. And the Marcus Corporation has promised to continue making improvements to the golf courses, which have already endured beyond the era of the Playboy Clubs. □

 **GRAND GENEVA RESORT & SPA**
Highway 50 East • Lake Geneva 53147 • 414/248-8811

**Directions:** Hwy. 50 east of Lake Geneva
**Course:** Brute, 18 holes/par 72/7,258 yards;
 Briar Patch, 18 holes/par 71/6,742 yards
**Fee:** $$$$   (Fee includes cart)

# Lake Arrowhead

*If you yearn for the whistle of golf balls among the whispering pines, you'll love Lake Arrowhead.*

There's something about golf among the pines that clears the head and invigorates a sputtering game. That something has long led wealthy Easterners to famed courses such as those in the sand hill region of Pinehurst, North Carolina.

If you yearn for the whistle of golf balls among the whispering pines, you don't have to travel to the South. You'll find it at Lake Arrowhead, in Wisconsin's sparsely populated "central sands" region. Nearby is the mighty Wisconsin River, which drains an area known by most summer visitors for its cranberries, paper mills and good fishing. Add championship golf to the list of attractions.

Lake Arrowhead Golf Course, part of a 3,000-acre vacation home development, has acquired a reputation as a prime golf destination and has consistently been rated among the top public courses in the country.

Designed by one-time partners Ken Killian and Dick Nugent, who designed Illinois' Kemper Lakes, Lake Arrowhead opened for play in two stages in the 1980s but without the fanfare that greeted other new state courses by "name" designers. Nevertheless, golfers soon discovered this out-of-the-way course, located 15 miles south of Wisconsin Rapids, and quickly sang its praises.

You, too, will find something to like in the lush fairways, large, undulating greens, sculptured bunkers, natural sandy areas and tall pines that typify Lake Arrowhead. The par-72, 6,624-yard course is spread over 130 wooded acres, and you often get the feeling of being alone because other fairways are hidden from view. With homesites and campsites tucked away in the pines, there's a feeling of seclusion.

Tee off on the fifth hole, and you'll get that feeling. The fairway of the 388-yard par 4 doglegs slightly to the right and then to the left. At the first bend, on the right, there's a trap that runs for more than 70 yards along the driving area. At the second bend, on the left, lies a big, sandy waste area. Ahead is a narrow opening to the long green, bounded on both sides by some of the course's 51 sand areas.

The 18th hole, a brutish 460 yards long, is considered by many to be the toughest on the course. Again, there's a feeling of seclusion among the pines and sand on this slight dogleg left. A 62-yard-long trap guards the right side of the landing area. Even if you hit the ball that far, you'll still need a long iron or fairway wood to safely reach the well-trapped, sloping green.

Three manmade lakes (in addition to 300-acre Lake Arrowhead), can come into play on five holes, giving variety to the wooded landscape. Most noteworthy of these is the par-5 ninth hole, perhaps Lake Arrowhead's premier hole. Running slightly downhill at the beginning, it sweeps right to left for 516 yards around a big lake, setting up an approach shot that's possibly over water and beach to a big green. Another good water hole is the tricky, par-3 fourth, a 140-yard hole running downhill from an elevated tee.

You'll find more variety on the 13th (par 4) and 14th (par 3) holes, which are set in a burned area of the jack pine and scrub oak forest. An out-of-control campfire burned over the area in the spring of 1980, when the holes were being designed. What remains is a recovering forest amid meadow grasses.

Designed as a fun course to play, Lake Arrowhead can be a bear from the back tees, especially for spray hitters. Homes along the course are set back in the woods, but the site boundaries—marked by out-of-bounds stakes—are very close to the rough in places, which means a stiff penalty for bad shots. It's best to keep the driver in the bag on the especially narrow corridors—if you can afford to sacrifice the distance.

Even if you're scoring poorly, take a deep breath and enjoy the wonderful surroundings. If you're finishing a round at dusk, you'll have the pleasure of sharing the course with the many white-tailed deer that populate the region.

After the round, there's the bonus of relaxing in Lake Arrowhead's beautiful clubhouse, which provides locker rooms, a lounge and restaurant for visiting golfers. (The pool, however, is off-limits to nonmembers.)

The serene setting belies the development's sometimes-troubled financial history. While a golf course was always planned for the development (which dates back to the early 1970s), money problems kept the original developer, N.E. Isaacson, from following through. Under new ownership, the course was built—one nine at a time—for a relative bargain of less than $1 million, according to former course superintendent Jeff Parks, whom many credit with making the course a reality.

Clearing of land began in the fall of 1979, and Parks came on board the following spring. The design required relatively little major landscaping (the sandy soil provided easy drainage), and the first nine opened for play in 1982. Course managers liked what they saw and gave Parks the go-ahead for the second nine.

"The front nine was a learning experience. Once the seeding took place, it was my baby," Parks said. "They gave me a free hand on the back."

The second nine opened in 1985. Since then, golfers—and potential vacation home buyers—have flocked to this remote region of the state for golf among the pines. By 1994, all 1,800 homesites in the development were to be sold, and the course was to come under the management of the landowners' association, according to Carl Landino, club manager for more than a decade.

The Lake Arrowhead development has finally matured, becoming a settlement of retirees and working commuters from Nekoosa and Wisconsin Rapids. And the association continues to look forward. Expansion of the clubhouse is being considered, and an additional 400 acres of land purchased in late 1993 has been set aside for "potential amenities"—possibly nine or 18 more holes of golf, according to Landino. Golfers will cheer if that happens and the new holes match the high standard set by the current track. □

## LAKE ARROWHEAD GOLF COURSE
1195 Apache Lane • Nekoosa 54457 • 715/325-2929

**Directions:** On Hwy. 13, 35 miles north of Wisconsin Dells,
   13 miles south of Wisconsin Rapids
**Course:** 18 holes/par 72/6,624 yards
**Fee:** $$$
**Amenities:** Full practice facilities; restaurant/lounge; tennis;
   pools; sauna; camping

# Lawsonia

*Golf Digest ranks the beautifully serene Lawsonia one of the top 75 public golfing facilities in the country.*

### The Links Course and the Woodlands Course

How can a 36-hole golf resort that's filled nearly to capacity every day of the season be so very quiet? With as many as 150 motorized carts in use at any one time, why are the twitter of birds and the rustle of pine branches predominant? Just what is it that makes the atmosphere on the courses at Lawsonia so downright serene?

Perhaps it's because these courses are located on the grounds of the American Baptist Assembly's Green Lake Conference Center, where such an atmosphere would be appreciated, if not demanded, by the visitors here on religious retreat. Or perhaps it's simply because the entire area surrounding the calm waters of Wisconsin's deepest lake is pastoral. Neon is scarce here. Crime might be defined as moving in on a buddy's favorite fishing spot.

No doubt it was the beauty and serenity that drew Victor Lawson here more than 100 years ago. The son of Norwegian immigrants, Lawson, who had turned a failing "penny journal" into the world-renowned Chicago Daily News, and his wife were frequent weekend visitors to the Green Lake area.

In 1888, the Lawsons bought a 10-acre tract—a place called Lone Tree Point, where Mrs. Lawson and a group of friends had been forced ashore by rough weather during a boating excursion. Over the next two decades, the Lawsons spent more than $8 million turning their modest retreat into a fabulous, 1,100-acre country estate. It included a nine-hole golf course, built mainly for the amusement of guests since Lawson rarely played the game himself.

Thus began Lawsonia, which Golf Digest magazine ranks among the top 75 public golfing facilities in the country.

After Lawson's death in 1924, the estate was sold to the H.O. Stone Realty Company of Chicago (for a bargain price of $300,000). The firm then spent $3 million to build an 18-hole golf course that replaced Lawson's original layout and to develop lots for private homes.

The course, opened in 1930, was designed by Chicago's William Langford and Theodore Moreau, who also designed Ozaukee Country

Club in Mequon and nine holes at West Bend Country Club. Touring pros, barnstorming through the Midwest in the 1930s, stopped to play the Little Lawsonia Open. Ben Hogan made the stop, as did Sam Snead. Byron Nelson shot 69 here in 1939, which was the course record at the time.

Lawsonia flourished until 1942, when World War II gas shortages forced the closing of the front nine. The Northern Baptist Convention bought the property in 1943, again for the sum of $300,000. When the front nine was reopened in 1946, the course was on its way to building the reputation it maintains today.

A third nine was opened in 1983, and a fourth in 1991. Both were designed by Georgia native Rocky Roquemore.

The original 18, now called the Links Course, has always been considered a difficult layout. Measuring 6,764 yards from the blue tees, it has a Scottish feel about it, with open, gently rolling fairways pocked with deep-faced bunkers. In contrast, the 6,618-yard Woodlands Course is cut into heavy woods and lies closer to the shores of Green Lake.

The second and third holes on the Woodlands Course are prime examples of both the beauty and terror that characterize this layout. Number 2, a par 4 of 341 yards from the back tee, works its way around the left side of an abandoned rock quarry. It's less than 230 yards to the quarry from the tee, so the best approach is to hit short, then play a shot of 120 to 130 yards to the green. A more dangerous route is to aim for the extension of the fairway off to the right of the quarry, which leaves a slightly shorter approach and a better angle to the green. Foolhardy golfers might even try to blast a tee shot around the trees at the corner, hoping for a bounce close to the green. If that's successful, large trees near the left front edge of the green make even a short pitch difficult from that side.

The green on No. 3 is 168 yards out and some 60 feet below the tee, making for both a terrific view and a muscle-tensing tee shot. Trees lie close to the left of the green, which is guarded by two large sand traps at the front and another in back. To the right is a steep drop-off toward the lake. So pretty. And so easy to make a 5 or 6.

The Woodlands Course has 75 sand traps, with water coming into play on four holes. The greens are big and well-contoured; fairways are lined with pines and assorted hardwoods.

The Links Course, while more open, is no less challenging. Many of its 61 sand traps—in the fairways and around the greens—have been built in a manner that makes it difficult to exit, except sideways. The greens are contoured and often elevated.

The green on the 161-yard, par-3 seventh hole gets its elevation from a boxcar buried beneath it. Missing the green on any side means big trouble; there are steep banks in front and on the sides, and tall trees to the rear.

The challenge on the par-3 10th hole is to reach a green that's 239 yards away. Many of us don't hit the ball that far—and that's not all bad here. It's better to be short than to hit into one of the long, narrow traps to the left and right of the green.

Nearly all the design characteristics on the Links Course are evident on the 13th hole, a par 5 of 568 yards from the back tee. Your drive must miss a big trap on the left and be followed with a second shot that stays to the right of a tree in the fairway, while stopping short of a valley in front of the green. The approach is a shot of 130 to 150 yards to a green that drops off sharply to the left.

A new clubhouse and restaurant, opened upon completion of the fourth nine in 1991, makes Lawsonia a destination resort.

The estate is used by the Baptist Assembly for meetings and conferences year round. Many of the private homes originally built on the property are rented as guest houses. Some are modest, while others—like the Anne Hathaway cottage, with seven bedrooms, five baths and private pier—are truly grand.

Remnants of the original Lawson estate are still in evidence. The main dairy barn, the largest barn in Wisconsin, is now an air-conditioned guest dormitory. Judson Tower, the largest of seven original water towers on the estate, has an observation deck 200 feet above Green Lake. Mrs. Lawson liked to take tea and entertain friends in a lounge she had built at the top of the tower. A large lighted cross now adorns the tower and, at night, can be seen for miles across the lake.

So welcome to Lawsonia—something Victor Lawson started for the benefit of his family and friends that has evolved into a special treat for all golfers to enjoy. □

## LAWSONIA
Highway 23 • Green Lake 54941 • 414/294-3320

**Directions:** Two miles west of Green Lake on Hwy. 23, Green Lake Conference Center
**Course:** Links Course, 18 holes/par 72/6,764 yards; Woodlands Course, 18 holes/par 72/6,618 yards
**Fee:** $$$$    (Fee includes cart)
**Amenities:** Restaurant; conference room; locker rooms; one of largest pro shops in Wisconsin

# Madeline Island

*Located on the shore of Chequamegon Bay, Madeline Island reminds some of a Scottish seaside course.*

Robert Trent Jones didn't design many courses like the cozy Madeline Island Golf Club.

The master architect designed a unique par-71 layout at La Pointe, on Lake Superior's Madeline Island, where the setting alone makes a trip to Wisconsin's northernmost reaches worthwhile. Many holes on the course share greens, tees and, in some cases, fairways. Only two holes, Nos. 7 and 16, fit the conventional mold of one tee, one fairway and one green.

Some regulars say the golf course reminds them of St. Andrews in Scotland. Indeed, Madeline Island Golf Club does have some of the feel of a Scottish seaside course. The 6,366-yard layout has the double greens and wide-open fairways of St. Andrews. And there's the wind—sometimes gentle, sometimes fierce, but rarely absent.

But this course lies on a heavily wooded and hilly Great Lakes island, not a flat and barren Scottish coastal plain. And relatively sheltered Chequamegon Bay is not the rugged North Sea—at least on most days.

Jones' efficient and compact layout was built amid pine, oak and maple trees on land provided by the late Theodore S. Gary. Gary, of a wealthy Twin Cities family that spent summers on the island, was a gentleman and sportsman who was crazy about golf, according to former associates. He envisioned building a fine golf course and clubhouse, along with a restaurant and marina, to entertain his rich friends, recalled Jerry Dunn, an island resident and part-time golf pro at the semiprivate club. Most of the plan came into being, but a large-scale vacation home development Gary hoped for did not. "There weren't enough people to make a going business," Dunn said.

"Ted's grand idea was to have lots of houses built along the course," said Robert Finnman, one of a score of original club members and part of a group that rescued the club from neglect in the early 1980s. "That really didn't take place."

It was too soon for something like that to happen. "He just wanted to do something for the island," Finnman added. "Money was no object."

Gary's project changed island life. He spent $6 million on the complex, including some $4 million on the course, according to Finnman. Jones began construction in 1965, and with the help of son Bobby and many truckloads of topsoil brought from the mainland, transformed the forest and part of an old nine-hole course into an 18-hole beauty.

The course's grand opening in 1968 was something to be remembered. Gary brought a big band and bagpipe players in from New York and ferried guests to the island on planes provided by corporate pals in the Twin Cities. "It was a full weekend deal," Finnman recalled.

But the development began to falter after Gary was divorced. The island property was eventually sold, and the course changed hands several times before Finnman, and others, formed the nonprofit corporation that rescued it in 1982. Today the club has fewer than 100 members but takes nonmember play arranged in advance.

Madeline Island has a 3,000-foot-long paved landing strip, but most visitors drive to picturesque Bayfield and board an auto ferry for the 20-minute ride across Chequamegon Bay. It's a trip reminiscent of a journey to New England's Cape Cod and its offshore islands, although Madeline Island and environs are far more low-key, despite establishment of an Indian-run gambling casino near Bayfield.

The water route from Bayfield to La Pointe has been traveled for centuries. La Pointe was an early fur-trading center, and the French affirmed its strategic importance in the 17th century by establishing an outpost here. The island is named for the daughter of Ojibway chief White Crane. She took the name Madeline when she married a fur trader in 1785. History buffs can visit the Madeline Island Historical Museum, which stands on the site of an old American Fur Company trading post near the ferry landing.

Madeline Island Golf Club offers spectacular views of La Pointe, the marina and nearby Indian burial ground, and the Wisconsin mainland. It also provides a challenge not often found on the average short-yardage resort layout.

The course features well-conditioned greens, which are big and rolling in the Jones style. Deep greenside bunkers are common. The par 4s are long and mostly uphill—four of 11 measure more than 400 yards from the back tees. Only one—the 322-yard 6th hole—is shorter than 350 yards.

The 6th hole and its companion, No. 15, are tricky. The two holes share a wood-lined fairway, then split off left and right to the greens. Number 6, a dogleg left, leaves a delicate approach shot, even if you manage to find the flat part of the landing area. The shot is uphill to an elevated, sloping, two-tiered green. On the 352-yard 15th, the approach is slightly downhill to a green that's perched on a bluff above Lake Superior.

Take time to pause at spots like the 15th green to glimpse sailboats skimming the blue-gray waters of the vast inland sea. It's likely that you'll have the time because the course is rarely crowded—especially in the often chilly off-season before May 15 and after September 15.

As the season winds down after Labor Day, and island life slows down even more, you can enjoy a brisk round in these beautiful surroundings at a lower rate. And you can ponder at just how lucky you are to be playing golf on an island in Lake Superior, on a course designed by Robert Trent Jones. □

 **MADELINE ISLAND GOLF COURSE**
P. O. Box 83 • La Pointe 54850 • 715/747-3212

**Directions:** North of Ashland on Hwy. 13, 15-minute ferry ride from Bayfield
**Course:** 18 holes/par 71/6,366 yards
**Fee:** $$$    Cart mandatory, not included in fee
**Amenities:** Pro shop; driving range; putting green; snack bar

# Mascoutin

*Any weakness with a putter or sand wedge
will be quickly exposed at Mascoutin.*

Mascoutin Golf Club is not the most difficult layout in the state—although any weakness with the putter or sand wedge will quickly be exposed here. Your children, however, will find this course much more demanding in years to come; their children may shake their heads and wonder who created this monster.

That's because Mascoutin has been engaged in an on-going tree-planting program. Since the course opened in 1975, nearly 2,000 trees have been planted. They've grown substantially, but are not as yet intimidating, except at the finishing holes, where the trees are formidable.

Someday, however, tall, mature trees will block openings that exist today, swallowing shots that now safely bounce through and turning slightly misdirected shots into double bogeys.

The course also has 65 sand traps—big ones, not just accents around the greens. The large, sloping greens are tough to read and tough to putt because of strategically placed knobs and knolls. Someday, Mascoutin will have this and big trees.

Mascoutin Golf Club lies just south of Berlin, on a hill overlooking the Fox River, where a tribe of fire-worshipping Indians called the Mascoutin lived more than three centuries ago. The business of tanning and sewing hides began here nearly 150 years ago, and Berlin today is known as Wisconsin's "fur and leather capital," with a host of local businesses producing furs, gloves, boots, moccasins and other leather products. The city of 5,400 is also noted for its elegant Victorian-style homes.

The original Mascoutin Golf Club was a nine-hole course located within Berlin's city limits. But when club members Dr. and Mrs. L.J. Seward donated 220 acres of land on which the new course was built, the old layout was parceled off as homesites.

Architect Lawrence Packard, assisted by his son, Roger, designed the new Mascoutin. The elder Packard's designs include several other highly regarded Wisconsin courses, among them Brown County Golf Course in Oneida, Naga-Waukee Golf Course in Pewaukee, Peninsula State Park Golf Course in Door County, and Stevens Point Country Club.

Roger Packard also lists several Wisconsin courses on his resume, including Timber Ridge in Minocqua and Trappers Turn in Wisconsin Dells (with Andy North).

Together the Packards produced a course at Mascoutin that's devoid of gimmicks but strong because of the variety of its holes.

The second hole, a short, manageable par 5 of 509 yards from the back tee, is followed by a long, difficult par 4 of 465 yards. Number 4 is a short par 3 of 158 yards, with a green that's almost completely surrounded by sand. The fifth hole is also short (346 yards) but has a tricky dogleg left to negotiate, with a sloping, well-trapped green.

The par-5 sixth hole offers a blind tee shot to the crest of a ridge, followed by a second shot down a natural gully. The third shot is uphill to another well-contoured green.

The smooth flow of the course continues on the back nine. A sharp dogleg to the right on No. 10, which is guarded by a cluster of sand traps, forces you to aim to the left, adding even more length to a hole that's substantially long already (406 yards from the back tee).

The 13th and 14th holes are side by side and radically different. Number 13 plays downhill to a green that's only 355 yards away, while No. 14 stretches uphill for 403 yards.

There are no easy routes back to the clubhouse from here. Mascoutin's finishing holes can best be described as a bit nasty. Number 15, a 412-yard par 4, has a narrow landing area off the elevated tee, with out-of-bounds on the left and a pond on the right. The approach shot, which can require anything from an 8-iron to a 2-iron, depending on the wind, is to an elevated green.

The 16th hole is a long par 5 of 549 yards, with a double turn to the left. The challenge comes on the second shot, where mature trees loom on the left and a pond guards the right. The hazards on both sides come into play quickly, and even a mid-iron lay-up shot requires accuracy. The green also proves to be a tough target because of two sand traps at the front. The 17th hole is a relatively short par 3 of 162 yards, but your tee shot must clear a pond and hold on a green with a hard back-to-front slope.

That leaves No. 18, a hole that will decide many a match. The fairway slopes left toward the woods with a row of oak trees on the right. For the best angle to the green, keep your tee shot to the right, but away from the oaks. The second shot is over water to a green that's guarded by sand in front and a large oak tree near the left front edge.

If you battle Mascoutin's final holes on even terms, you can walk off the 18th green with the satisfaction of knowing you've passed a tough test of golf—a test that will get tougher every year. □

# MASCOUTIN GOLF CLUB
County Trunk A • Berlin 54923 • 414/361-2360

**Directions:** From Milwaukee, Hwy. 41 north to Hwy. 23 west to Green Lake, Hwy. 49 north seven miles, then left on Co. A
**Course:** 18 holes/par 72/6,821 yards
**Fee:** $$$   (Fee includes cart)
**Amenities:** PGA staff; pro shop; golf range; lessons; restaurant; dinner/golf packages

# Naga-Waukee

*Situated near beautiful Pewaukee Lake, Naga-Waukee is "a very lovely place."*

Lawrence Packard, Course Designer

If ever a piece of property were suited for golf, it's the land golfers know as Naga-Waukee. You only need to step up to the 14th tee at Naga-Waukee Golf Course to know why.

Spread out before you is a 542-yard, double-dogleg par 5 that winds down a forested hill toward beautiful Pewaukee Lake, which is dotted with sailboats on most summer days. Regardless of your score to this point, the exhilarating view makes you feel as if you can hit the drive of your life. Even if you don't, the stroll down the fairway is a scenic pleasure.

Lawrence Packard designed this jewel. Of course, the well-known architect had a great piece of property with which to work. The lakes and rolling countryside are the product of the last great glacier, which advanced to about this point more than 10,000 years ago.

Waukesha County officials showed a high degree of foresight when they bought 200 acres of the old Audley farm for $55,000, back when Pewaukee "probably was considered to be out in the boondocks," said course professional Peter Schlicht. The par-72, 6,772-yard course opened in 1966, taking its name from lakes Nagawicka and Pewaukee. "It's a very, very lovely place," recalled Packard, who has designed several pretty and playable Wisconsin courses.

The prime real estate surrounding the golf course is today sought by developers and conservationists, all of whom appreciate the value of a spectacular view amid the growing sprawl moving east from Milwaukee. The Ice Age Trail, a federal footpath that follows the glacier's advance, crosses nearby hills and dales. To the south and north of the course is the Kettle Moraine State Forest, named for features that typify the glaciated landscape. Interstate 94, which runs east-west between Milwaukee and Madison, provides easy access to it all.

In designing Naga-Waukee, Packard took advantage of the natural features and made it fit the mold he favors for municipal courses—forgiving but challenging. You'll find relatively wide landing areas, big rolling greens and lots of leafy trees in a parklike atmosphere. The sand traps are big, but they usually mean trouble for only the most errant of shots.

"It's a course you never get tired of playing," Schlicht said.

Testimony to that is the heavy play, which sometimes makes it tough for noncounty residents to get a tee time during the peak playing season. Be patient, and you'll be rewarded with an opportunity to play a well-maintained and pretty course that keeps you thinking.

Shotmaking is the key to keeping your score low at Naga-Waukee. Position your drives correctly, and you'll find open avenues to the green. Misplace the tee shot, and you'll find yourself in trouble.

The trouble is water on the tough fourth hole, a 427-yard dogleg right, which has a pond stretching along most of the right side. It's sand on the fifth hole, a 362-yard, right-angle par 4 with three big traps at the corner. And more sand on the eighth, a tricky, 144-yard par 3 with three large greenside bunkers. Trees are the trouble on holes like the No. 7, a subtly difficult, 365-yard, uphill par 4 with a dogleg right that's wooded along the entire right side.

But it's the back nine where the terrain and shotmaking get really interesting. Beginning on the 411-yard 10th hole, a dogleg right bounded by trees, you must do more than hit and hope. To achieve par, you'll need to place your drive on the flat, open landing area in the left-center fairway before it drops off into a steep ravine. The second shot must cross the ravine.

The drive is also key on Nos. 14 and 15. Fourteen, the scenic hole that drops toward Pewaukee Lake, is a potential birdie hole—if you set it up with a drive to a level spot on the left side. Slice to the woods on the right side, and it will likely be a bogey hole. The same goes for the 15th hole, a 362-yard, uphill par 4. Par becomes much easier with a drive to the level spot at the dogleg's left-hand turn. But hit into one of three deep bunkers at the corner, and you're probably looking at bogey—or worse.

On other holes, you may want to put away the driver and use a long iron to make sure you find the fairway. Number 11, a 503-yard par 5, is the leading example of the benefits of playing it smart. For the blind tee shot, hit an iron to the top of the tree-lined ridge while avoiding the big trap on the right side, 230 yards from the green. From there, you'll be able to see the rest of the hole. Two more irons can get you home.

Club selection is also paramount on the 16th hole, a 179-yard par 3. The four tee boxes offer a grand view of Pewaukee Lake and the hole, which lies on a ledge far below tee level. Use a couple of clubs less than you normally would for the distance and this could be a birdie hole. However, you must avoid the traps to the right and left and trouble behind the green, where a severe slope leads to a small grove of trees.

The 17th and 18th holes, both par 4s, are less tricky and scenic but no place to let your guard down if you're working on a good score. The 17th is a long, par-4 dogleg right of 427 yards. The 18th hole is considerably shorter but requires an accurate drive to avoid small trees on the inside of the dogleg.

If you tend to be distracted by pretty natural surroundings, thinking your way around Naga-Waukee isn't easy. But it will help you stay closer to par. □

 **NAGA-WAUKEE GOLF COURSE**
1897 Maple Avenue • Pewaukee 53072 • 414/367-2153

**Directions:** I-94 to exit 290, west on Frontage Road to Co. E, then north one-half mile
**Course:** 18 holes/par 72/6,722 yards
**Fee:** $$$

# New Richmond

*A course that looks mature beyond its years, with bluegrass fairways that shine in the summer sun.*

Golf is an 18-hole game, right? Tom Doar thought so. He also thought that a 75-acre parcel of farmland adjoining New Richmond Golf Club would be a perfect spot for expanding the cozy, nine-hole layout.

Not everyone agreed. The property owner was willing to sell, but in 1965 the New Richmond Golf Club's board of directors determined that the club couldn't afford to buy the land. Doar, an attorney whose home stands beside the course's second hole, cared deeply about the future of the golf club, and he brooded about the club's decision not to buy the land for expansion.

"Finally I thought, maybe I could get some of the people who supported the idea to join with me," he said. "We'd buy it and sort of hold it for the golf club."

Doar and six friends did just that. They also decided to plant some trees because a good golf course needs trees. Through a government tree planting program, they bought evergreen seedlings and had them planted at a cost of about one cent apiece.

Shortly after Doar and his group purchased the land, Doar received an office visit from a man named Don Herfort, who had legal business in New Richmond. Herfort, a Green Bay native, was a former accountant at 3M in Minneapolis and had designed the company's golf course. By the time he met Doar, Herfort had other design projects going, so he introduced himself as a golf course architect.

Talk about serendipity! Doar had Herfort lay out a master plan for an 18-hole course at New Richmond Golf Club. Then Doar and his friends began planting their evergreen seedlings more strategically, along what might someday be fairways and greens.

Now jump forward to the early 1980s. New Richmond Golf Club decided to go ahead with the expansion. With city backing (the course is owned by the city of New Richmond but is operated entirely by its membership), the club borrowed $300,000 to build nine new holes.

The club also needed a bit more land. The idea was to use only a portion of Doar's 75-acre parcel for the golf course—perhaps enough to build five or six holes—and sell the rest as homesites.

John Doar, Tom's brother, who owned property to the east of the existing course on the far side of the Willow River, donated land for the remaining three holes.

Herfort, whose design credits include the highly regarded North-Wood Golf Club in Rhinelander, returned in 1982 to refine his earlier plan. He used holes 1, 2 and 3 from the old course, then added new holes—4, 5, 6 and 7 near the river. Existing holes were used to make Nos. 8 through 12, and Herfort designed six new holes, 13 through 18, on the land donated by Tom Doar's group—now forested with 30,000 17- and 18-year-old evergreens of various types.

The net result is a course that looks mature beyond its years, with bluegrass fairways that shine in the summer sun. It's challenging enough to have earned a slope rating of 136—fifth-highest in the state.

The golf club has a full membership and a long waiting list. With the Twin Cities less than 30 minutes away, the course is popular with Minnesotans. Yet, it's still possible for the daily fee player to get a tee time and experience one of the most enjoyable courses in western Wisconsin.

With three sets of tees, the par-72 course plays from 6,716 yards down to 5,547 yards. Perhaps the most challenging and beautiful section of the course includes holes four through seven, which stretch over the Willow River.

Number 4 is a dogleg right of 372 yards from the back tee. The drive must be kept to the left side of the fairway to allow for an open approach across a wide spot in the river to a sloping, heart-shaped green guarded by sand traps and trees.

On the difficult, 409-yard fifth hole, the tree-lined river runs along the right side of the fairway from tee to green. There's also a pond on the left that can come into play. A drive favoring the right side of the fairway offers the best look at the green.

Number 6 is a 506-yard par 5, with trees lining both sides of the fairway. You'll need two accurate shots to get into position to fire at the crowned, well-bunkered green.

The river comes back into play on No. 7, a par 3 of 194 yards. With the river in front and two big traps around an elevated, terraced green, par is a significant achievement here—as it is on any of the holes in this section of the course.

The final six holes feature rolling terrain and lots of pine trees. Number 16 is a 500-yard par 5 that's pinched in the middle by two large sand traps. The long, narrow green is cupped by two traps in front and crowded by woods in back.

The course has a seamless quality, which speaks well for Herfort's work. The only sign that the course was built piecemeal is that it doesn't come back to the clubhouse after nine holes. Instead, the "turn" is at the 12th hole, a pretty par 3 backed by a bed of flowers.

New Richmond Golf Club might have been content to continue as a nine-hole course forever. But Tom Doar and a few others believed their club should have an 18-hole course. With determination, patience and a spirit of generosity, they made it happen. □

 **NEW RICHMOND GOLF COURSE**
1226 180th Avenue • New Richmond 54017 • 715/246-6724

**Directions:** One-half mile west of New Richmond on Hwy. 64
**Course:** 18 holes/par 72/6,716 yards
**Fee:** $$$
**Amenities:** Pro shop; grill; driving range

# NorthWood

*With narrow fairways cut into a dense forest, NorthWood demands accuracy.*

From the first tee at Rhinelander's NorthWood Golf Club, it's possible to see the state bird (robin), the state tree (sugar maple), maybe even the state animal (white-tailed deer). But it's impossible to ignore the fact that the trees—state sanctioned or not—are uncomfortably close to the edges of the fairway.

This majestic forest from which the course was hewn is home to an abundance of native flora and fauna.

It's also a graveyard for thousands of little white Maxiflis, Ultras and Titleists! In 1989, when the course was new, Minneapolis architect Don Herfort explained that the tightness of the fairways was intentional but not necessarily permanent. As timber was removed during construction, trees that were once deep in the forest became exposed to more sunshine and wind. Some would die because of this change in their environment, causing a natural widening of the playing area.

But that didn't happen—at least, not enough to help players who stray on the tee shot. This is still a course that demands accuracy, particularly on the drive. In many places, the woods are too dense to allow for much hope of recovery.

By the time they reach the back nine, prudent players have usually devised some semiworkable plan to keep the ball in play. Here's a tip from head professional Dan Buckley: Approach each hole like a par 3. Aim for the landing area off the tee as if it were the green on a par 3. (The landing areas, however small, are still bigger than the greens.) From there, aim for the green as if it were another par 3. Play par 5s like they're two par 3s plus a chip. This is good advice because the height of the trees makes it virtually impossible to cut doglegs. And trying to bend shots around corners often leads to landing areas that are narrower and more difficult.

Prudence pays off on a hole like No. 7. It's a good idea to forsake the driver on this par 5. Use a long iron or fairway wood off the tee to reach the largest landing area. A blast from a good player's driver will find a much tighter spot that falls off left toward a marshy area.

The hole provides a splendid view from the tee boxes, which

overlook the fairway at treetop level. You'll also see a boulder that's roughly the size of a small shed standing in the middle of the fairway. But from the height of the tee area, a shot of about 165 yards will easily clear it.

After a few holes, your fear of the forest's dangers will fade as you tune in to the beauty of the bluegrass fairways and bentgrass greens. Relax. Enjoy the course. It's one of northern Wisconsin's finest.

NorthWood Golf Club was, for years, a good idea waiting to happen. Rhinelander's city fathers had discussed building a municipal course over a span of more than 20 years, but the plans never seemed to materialize. Then Paul Cooper took the initiative. Authorized by the mayor to seek land on which to build the course, Cooper, a former superintendent at Rhinelander Country Club, contacted the board of directors of the Wausau Paper Company, parent firm of the Rhinelander Paper Company.

After several months of diligent work, Cooper's efforts paid off. Selecting an 800-acre parcel, Wausau Paper told course designer Herfort to pick whichever 260 acres he needed for the course.

While Herfort's name might not have the marquee value of a Pete Dye or a Robert Trent Jones, he can design a beautiful, challenging golf course that can be built for about the same amount of money that Jack Nicklaus gets to sign his name on a contract.

NorthWood was built for less than the $1.5 million the city had budgeted for it. The key to staying within the budget, Herfort said, is to plan well. "It's like Mount Rushmore. You don't just go up there and start carving a guy's face," he said. "You have to know that a nose is going to be seventeen and a half feet long, so you have to have a drawing ahead of time. It's the same way with a golf course. I make very detailed grading plans, green drawings and trap drawings, and I expect the contractors to come up with what I have on the plans. That way they don't have to do the same work two or three times."

There's a rugged, northern Wisconsin feel to the entire par-72 layout, which measures 6,719 yards from the back tees. The forest frames nearly every fairway and green, providing a sense of solitude on each hole. Deer are regular visitors. Black bears have been seen early in the spring, but they hightail it when the golfers start arriving. There was even a moose hanging around during construction of the course.

The focal point of the course is an irregularly shaped pond—actually a partially dredged bog that's part open water, part marsh grass and cattails—that's surrounded by the 11th, 12th and 17th holes. The 11th hole is a par 3 of 142 yards from the elevated championship tee to a narrow green perched on a peninsula. Club selection is all-important here, and can range from a long iron to a wedge depending on the wind.

The drive on No. 12 must fly at least 190 yards from the back tee to clear the pond that edges in from the left. This still leaves a fairly long second shot to a green that falls off sharply toward the marshy pond.

The fairway on the 17th hole actually hooks around a finger of the pond that's not visible from the tee. A good drive leaves an approach shot of about 150 yards, over water to a green that slopes back to front.

A 30-foot-high, manmade waterfall is visible from all three holes and provides a pleasant touch to this corner of the course.

Each hole at NorthWood has its own personality, yet certain design characteristics prevail throughout the course. Many holes feature large sand traps on either side of the green, but there's nearly always a front opening that allows for run-up shots. And while the ever-present birch, maple and spruce surround most greens, the trees are set back so that a shot can take a bounce or two off the back of the green and still be playable. Nearly every green has some degree of slope. Many are contoured in a saddle shape—high on the sides and low front and back.

Buckley, the pro, says the course is not as intimidating after the first round or two—if you're hitting the ball pretty well. If not, "it can be a bear," he said. The number of balls buried in the wooded graveyard attest to that. □

## NORTHWOOD GOLF COURSE
6301 Highway 8 West • Rhinelander 54501 • 715/282-6565

**Directions:** Three miles west of Rhinelander on Hwy. 8
**Course:** 18 holes/par 72/6,719 yards
**Fee:** $$
**Amenities:** Pro shop; snack bar; driving range

# Old Hickory

*Stately and mature, Old Hickory is surrounded by trees–poplar, oak and, of course, hickory.*

Take a moment at Old Hickory Country Club simply to enjoy the setting.

The seventh tee is a good spot for this moment of intimacy. Off to the right you'll see a still pond, covered with floating lily pads. The single blue heron who claims this spot as home seems oblivious to the intrusion of golf carts or the thwack of Ping against Titleist. Grass in the meadow beyond moves softly in the breeze. Trees abound—poplar, oak, hickory, their leaves shimmering in the rays of the morning sun.

While the pond lies between you and the green, it's not a frightening hazard. The carry is little more than 100 yards from the back tee on this 135-yard par 3 and considerably less from the forward tee. The green is pitched helpfully toward you, and the land around rises gently, like a pleasant outdoor amphitheater. Just beyond is a barbecue pit—a reminder that this would be a wonderful spot for a picnic.

Welcome to Old Hickory—a stately and mature golf course located two and a half miles east of Beaver Dam, in the south-central section of the state.

Old Hickory opened as a nine-hole course in 1920. It was designed by Tom Bendelow, a Scotsman and prolific architect whose Wisconsin credits include such well-known and beautiful courses as Tripoli Country Club in Milwaukee, Blue Mound Country Club in Wauwatosa, Chenequa Country Club in Hartland, Big Foot Country Club in Fontana, Oshkosh Country Club and Racine Country Club. Old Hickory remained a nine-hole layout until 1968, when a second nine was built under the direction of Billy Sixty, the legendary golf writer for the Milwaukee Journal. Some existing holes were altered during the expansion, but the new course retained much of the varied flavor of the original.

Old Hickory has long, difficult holes and short, easy holes, big greens and tiny greens, rolling terrain and flat stretches, open fairways and fairways lined with trees.

Perhaps the most difficult hole on the course—certainly one of the most scenic—is No. 14, a par 4 of 393 yards from the middle tee, with a dogleg of almost 90 degrees that effectively eliminates any easy path to par.

The tee shot is down a corridor lined left and right by trees, with a big pond that stretches all the way along the fairway and around behind the green. It's easy to visualize a high, sweeping drive that just misses the trees and settles softly in the fairway—out of sight from the tee but a comfortable short-iron shot from the green. Easy to visualize, not so easy to execute.

It's much more prudent to hit a mid-iron straightaway, but less than 185 yards since the water will catch anything longer. It's still 200 yards from the middle of the fairway to a green guarded left, right and back by an extension of the pond. Good luck!

Old Hickory's 1968 addition was built on farmland that still contained rocks—big rocks. Rather than cart the rocks away, course developers piled them in a neat row at the neck of the fairway on No. 4. While not actually encroaching on the fairway of this 501-yard par 5, they are, nevertheless, cause for concern on the approach to the green. Errant shots, as is frequently proven, bounce a long way off big rocks.

Several holes offer risk and reward challenges. Number 8, for example, is an inviting little par 4 of barely 300 yards from an elevated tee. The green is tucked around the corner to the right and could conceivably be reached from the tee by those whose knuckles drag upon the ground when they walk. But with trees along the right side (and water, too), the odds are better if you play the hole as designed. Use a long iron or fairway wood off the tee and follow up with a little wedge shot over the sand traps in front of the green.

The 16th hole, a 531-yard par 5 with a sharp left turn a couple of hundred yards out, is even more alluring. There are small trees and three sand traps at the corner, but it's possible to cut off some significant yardage here. Even a shot that finds the rough might yield an open look at the green. Or might not. Risk and reward.

The green on No. 10 looks terribly small, even after a long, well-placed tee shot to the right side of the fairway. That is, it would look terribly small if you could actually see it. Usually only the flagstick is visible from the fairway. The green sits on a shelf, well above the fairway, and is snuggled in close to the property line at the back and on the left. A high, soft second shot is necessary here.

The tee on No. 11 is even higher than the elevated 10th green, making the hole look shorter than its 413 yards. After launching a drive from cloud level, you descend a stairway made of railroad ties to face the rest of the hole uphill. It's a straightforward hole but tough because of the length.

The 18th is the longest hole on the course and was two short par 4s on the original nine-hole layout. Now it's a behemoth of 577 yards from the back tee. The fairway, level for the first half, takes on a significant left to right slant the rest of the way to the green. Keeping the second shot out of the right rough can be tricky.

It may well require a turn or two around Old Hickory to learn the safest places to be on the greens. Several greens have some nasty pitch to them. You'll three-putt if you challenge these slopes, and you'll have a devil of a time trying to hold a pitch from behind the green.

Old Hickory Country Club has been open to the public since the 1970s. The club built a driving range in 1990 and completed extensive remodeling of the clubhouse in 1993.

Roger Maltbie, of the PGA Tour, is a frequent visitor to Old Hickory, in part because his brother-in-law is a member. But maybe, like the rest of us, he also enjoys a quiet, natural course of unmatched beauty. □

**OLD HICKORY COUNTRY CLUB**
W7596 Highway 33 East • Beaver Dam 53916 • 414/887-7577

**Directions:** 2 1/2 miles east of Beaver Dam on Hwy. 33
**Courses:** 18 holes/par 72/6,667 yards
**Fee:** $$$
**Amenities:** Pro shop; snack bar

# Peninsula State Park

*The stretch of Green Bay shoreline containing the golf course and park is among the most scenic of all the beautiful spots in Door County.*

Only one Wisconsin state park can boast of a golf course. And only one Wisconsin golf course can boast of a totem pole—*and* a 69-yard, cliff-to-green par 3.

This is Peninsula State Park Golf Course, situated in one of Wisconsin's most popular recreation spots—the rugged Door Peninsula. Part of a massive dolomite ledge that loops eastward to form the falls at Niagara, the peninsula is bounded by Lake Michigan on the east and the lake's Green Bay on the west. It offers lovely settings for camping, hiking, biking, sailing and, of course, golf.

The stretch of Green Bay shoreline containing the golf course and park is among the most scenic of all the beautiful spots in Door County, with a spectacular view of Eagle Harbor and the village of Ephraim. The original Norwegian settlers, state park officials and course founders evidently recognized a prime piece of real estate when they saw it.

"The finest farm on the peninsula, and perhaps in all of Wisconsin, was the old Hanson farm, across the harbor from Ephraim. It had rich, deep soil, well drained, and was protected from strong winds by high, wooded hills on the north, west and south sides. There was never a crop failure on this farm. In addition, it had an unsurpassed scenic location. It is now no longer a farm but a first-class golf course in Peninsula State Park."

That passage is from *Old Peninsula Days*, a book of local history written by peninsula resident Hjalmar R. Holand, first published in 1925. As Holand tells it, the Hansons settled here in 1854, cleared the land, planted many apple trees, and operated the first profitable farm in the county. The state acquired the land in the early 1900s, paying ill-tempered Olaf Hanson a mere $8,000 (about $1,000 of which went to a Green Bay lawyer), according to Holand. "Could anyone blame Olaf for being sore?" Holand writes. By 1910, the state had acquired the lion's share of the park's 3,800 acres for about $80,000.

In 1921, a six-hole course was opened on the old Hanson farm—laid out by W.R. Lovekin of Green Bay on land leased from the state by the Ephraim Men's Club, according to a history published by the Peninsula Golf Associates, the nonprofit group that helps the Department of Natural Resources maintain the course. In 1926, the course added three more holes—these laid out by Alex Cunningham, the first course pro. In 1929-30, the course was expanded to the wooded plateau high above the first six and became an 18-hole layout.

It was in 1926 that Peninsula's trademark eighth hole—a 69-yarder over a chalky, 50-foot-high cliff—came into being. While much has changed in the ensuing years, old No. 8 remains untouched. The trademark hole is so favored by visitors that it could never be changed, said Walter Ellmann, a longtime club manager.

Another constant at this quirky little resort course—now a 6,216-yard, par-71 track—is the totem pole. Set between the first and ninth fairways, the 40-foot totem marks the grave of Potawatomi Chief Simon Kahquados, "a true and worthy Indian," according to the inscription on a nearby stone. The original pole, erected in 1927, was replaced in 1970 by a replica carved by summer resident Adlai Hardin. The black bear atop the pole is a clan symbol for the Potawatomi tribe.

Lawrence Packard, who designed several fine Wisconsin public courses, did a major redesign at Peninsula in the early 1960s, creating 11 new or drastically changed holes. Number 8, of course, was left intact. Packard, who has spent some summers in Door County, recalled designing three new holes for the wooded upper plateau.

Since then, the Peninsula Golf Associates group has continued to make improvements, although not always according to Packard's master plan, said Ellmann. The group recently used profits from their clubhouse and other concession operations to pay for new greens on Nos. 1 and 7.

Despite all of the changes over the years, including eliminating part of the course that crossed busy Highway 42, Peninsula State Park Golf Course maintains the look and feel of a bygone era, when courses weren't always manicured like a suburban lawn. You'll see old stone fences, play off lumpy fairways, and find holes with tiny greens and no sand traps. The hilly course often winds through deep peninsula forests of maple, pine and cedar. Along the way, you'll find picture-perfect views of Eagle Harbor and Ephraim.

Some of the loveliest views come on the 12th and 17th holes, perhaps the best holes on the course.

The 12th, a par 4 of 394 yards, is an uphill dogleg left featuring a tiny landing area that's unseen from the tee. The second shot is uphill to a green cut into a steep hillside. Miss left, and your ball could roll a long way down the grassy slope, leaving another full approach shot.

The 17th hole takes advantage of that same steep hillside. A par 3 of 179 yards from the back tee, it's all downhill to a comparatively level green backed up by trees. The view here is breathtaking. On a clear day, you can see over Eagle Harbor, past Ephraim, and up the coastline into the upper end of Lake Michigan's Green Bay.

The beauty is what draws golfers and tourists to the course and park—especially during the peak season between July 4th and Labor Day. In all, some 60,000 nine-hole rounds of golf are played in that short season. If you arrive in the off season and the clubhouse isn't open, you'll find a box in which to deposit your green fees or a donation. Old Olaf Hanson won't get a cut, but it'll help keep up a golf course that Wisconsin residents should be proud to own. □

## PENINSULA STATE PARK GOLF COURSE
Highway 42 • P.O. Box 218 • Fish Creek 54212 • 414/854-5791

**Directions:** Three miles north of Fish Creek on Hwy. 42
**Course:** 18 holes/par 71/6,224 yards
**Fee:** $$

# Rainbow Springs

*Sand traps are not a problem here because there are none.*

Don't expect the ordinary when you travel to Rainbow Springs Golf Club in Mukwonago. Rainbow Springs has been surprising people since the early 1960s.

At first it was the speed at which the main 18-hole course, Big Moraine, nicknamed "Big Mo," was made: 143 days, according to course historians.

In the ensuing years, when the 920-acre resort surrounding Big Mo fell on hard times, it was the absolute neglect that shocked—an impressive northwoods-style lodge and a massive hotel-convention center wasting away on a secluded piece of natural real estate near the southern Kettle Moraine State Forest. Visitors still are struck with an eerie feeling when they drive over the covered bridge, round a bend, and come into a scene that looks like the set for a horror movie. "The Resort That Wasn't," summed up one headline writer.

Perpetually under new management (the latest owner is a Los Angeles-based investment group that bought the site for $4.2 million in early 1994), the golf courses survive somehow despite bitter words said to be uttered by the initial developer, Francis Schroedel: "My ghost will haunt Rainbow Springs after I'm gone. It will never open without me."

But don't let all of this scare you from trying Big Mo and its companion 18-hole executive course, "Little Mo," two courses that play tougher than they appear.

Set amid a wild chunk of low-lying hills, marshland and forest formed by the passage of glaciers more than 10,000 years ago, Big Mo and Little Mo are definitely something different.

Sand traps aren't a problem here because there are none. But plenty of trouble lurks in the form of water, narrow fairways and thick underbrush. Water hazards are just about everywhere the glaciers and Schroedel put them, and they come into play on 14 holes.

Two of the toughest holes on Big Mo, a par-72 layout playing at 6,912 yards from the back tees, fly the Jolly Roger on their flagsticks. On these holes especially, Nos. 12 and 15, you'll understand why Big

Mo deserves its relatively high slope rating of 132.

Despite the financial problems that bedeviled the resort, turning it into a virtual ghost town, the main golf course has been a hard-to-beat track since its earliest days. The Women's Western Open, once a regular stop on the Ladies Professional Golf Association Tour, was played at Rainbow Springs in 1966. Hall-of-famer Mickey Wright won the $1,500 first prize with a four-round total of 302—the highest winning total by far on the tour that year.

A lot of golf balls have been lost in the water at Rainbow Springs since then. And a lot of money and speculation have chased the dream of Francis Schroedel. Schroedel, a wealthy Milwaukee developer, hoped to build a complete and luxurious resort on land he and his buddies had used for a hunting and fishing retreat. His first project was to build a lodge. From modest early plans it evolved into something much grander. By the time it opened on New Year's Day, 1959, at what was then known as the Rainbow Springs Hunting, Skeet and Trap Club, it featured 42 guest rooms, two dining rooms and an indoor pool.

Guests at the year-round club suggested a golf course. Schroedel seized the idea and built one at a breakneck pace in 1962 from his own design. On the heels of that came a 756-room hotel and a 90,000-square-foot convention center—all built with the finest materials. But their doors were opened only briefly to the public because Schroedel became mired in a financial bind.

By 1966, Schroedel's grandiose project began to slide because of mounting debts. Schroedel fought bitterly to retain control until 1973 when he finally lost the property through foreclosure. He died in 1976 at the age of 67, still dreaming the dream. It was on eviction day in late 1973 when Schroedel uttered the vow that his ghost would "haunt" Rainbow Springs, wife Anita told an interviewer in the late 1980s.

Since Schroedel, there have been a succession of failed resurrection attempts. Somehow Big Mo and Little Mo kept chugging along, hosting golfers drawn by curiosity and the desire to play in an out-of-the-way place where geese, cranes and other wildlife abound.

Things seemed to be changing for the better, when a company called TBM Management took over operation of Rainbow Springs in 1992. The management team, led by experienced golf managers Terry Anton and Jack Gaudion, brought improved maintenance, renewed promotion and a heralded juniors program that has featured a clinic by PGA Tour star Payne Stewart, a friend of Anton's.

The management also instituted innovative ways to speed play, such as fore caddies on the first hole to help locate the sometimes errant first shot and the offer of a free beer or soft drink for those who complete their round in four hours or less.

It also introduced skull-and-crossbones flags. And once you played the course, there were times you wanted to wave a white flag in surrender to the Jolly Roger.

Although the front nine is relatively open, there is water present on all but one hole—enough to require the golfer to keep his attention on the task at hand. Most of the course's drama, however, is on the back nine.

After a long but fairly docile par-5 10th hole, you travel into golf wilderness for a set of testing holes that has caused players to curse. No. 11 is a 215-yard par 3 with little room to maneuver the ball, meaning the long iron or fairway wood off the tee had better be straight. No. 12 is a 440-yard par 4 that evokes cries of "unfair" from many. But you'll rejoice if you somehow achieve par. The tee shot requires a long draw over and around a steep, tree-covered mound left by glaciers. If you miss, you'll likely end up in the creek that runs along the right side or in a nasty spot in the scrub brush that covers the hill. Even if you find a flat, playable lie, the second shot to the slightly elevated green still requires a mighty effort.

Nos. 13 and 14 are relative breathers but not so much that par is guaranteed. Then comes No. 15, a 518-yard par 5. Like No. 12, the drive is all important here. You must clear the creek that crosses in front of you and continues down the right side. If you bail out far enough to the right, you may find the landing area that you should have played on No. 12. The rest of No. 15 is uphill to a green that has brush and woods to the left and to the rear.

After another tough par 3—a pond is dangerously close on the right—you'll emerge to play the more open and conventional two finishing holes, hopefully with your score and dignity intact and pleasantly surprised that golf can survive the vagaries of the resort business. □

## RAINBOW SPRINGS GOLF COURSE
S103 W33599 Highway 99 • Mukwonago 53149 • 414/363-4550

**Directions:** Thirty miles west of Milwaukee's Mitchell Field airport, 1 1/2 hours north of Chicago
**Course:** Big Mo, 18 holes/par72/6,912 yards; Little Mo, 18 holes/par 65/4,253 yards
**Fee:** $$$   (Fee includes cart)
**Amenities:** Bar; grill; pro shop; PGA member; professional staff

# SentryWorld

*"Very possibly my Mona Lisa."*  Robert Trent Jones II, Course Designer

John W. Joanis had a penchant for doing things in a big way. But the insurance company executive may have outdone himself when it came to SentryWorld.

Joanis, then president of Stevens Point-based Sentry Insurance Company and the impetus behind this central Wisconsin gem, is said to have wanted "instant tradition" from his golf course.

Robert Trent Jones II, who designed the course, called his creation "very possibly my Mona Lisa." While it has yet to host the major tournament once envisioned for it, SentryWorld is a golf course that can be held up as a work of art—a treat to see and a treat to play.

Nowhere is that more apparent than on No. 16, the famed flower hole, which in itself may be worth the price of admission. The par 3 plays 177 yards from the back tees and 108 yards from the front. Even without the 90,000 flowers that decorate it, this signature hole would be highly regarded. The large, slightly elevated green is protected by three substantial traps. The heart-shaped putting surface slopes significantly from back to front, turning all but a precision tee shot into a possible three-putt.

The flower hole, which was Joanis' idea, is the most striking example of what Jones called his thematic approach to golf design.

"When a course is properly done, there's a completeness to the theme. SentryWorld is the flower theme—low-lying, relatively flat course, lakes, flowers and rocks," said Jones, calling the project a favorite of his. "I let the land reveal its secrets to me and then design to the land."

The flower hole is the opener in a trio of fine finishing holes that combine beautiful landscaping and terrific golf. Number 17 is a testy, downhill dogleg—a 415-yard par 4 that tempts the big driver into trouble with trees or water. The 18th—a brawny, 452-yard par 4 that's uphill all the way—will likely leave you gasping.

Joanis' quest for "instant tradition" didn't come cheap. A globetrotting, 14-handicap golfer who died in 1985, Joanis spent an estimated $10 million in corporate funds to transform 270 acres of swamp and woodland into the golf course and adjacent sports complex that's enjoyed by both company employees and visitors. So what if some insurance regulators saw it as endangering the company's financial health?

"He had an ego the size of King Kong," Lee Sherman Dreyfus once said of Joanis, his long-time friend. Dreyfus, a former governor, worked briefly for Sentry after leaving the governor's mansion in 1982.

"It's the kind of course God would have created had He had the money," Dreyfus joked.

"It was his baby," recalled former course superintendent Bill Roberts. "John Joanis wanted the best golf course he could get. The only thing he couldn't get was 50 years of tradition."

SentryWorld opened amid much hoopla in the summer of 1982. Most critics gave it rave reviews, and the course quickly made its way onto the lists of the nation's best public courses.

"This golf course was built to make a profit, and it will be operated to make a profit," Joanis crowed to the press at the course opening.

He also wanted the course to host a professional golf tournament. "But I would be careful about bringing in an event," Joanis said. "The course must stay as it was built. If anybody touches that course, I'll break his head." But he did reverse the numbering of the holes after the course opened, presumably to better showcase the picturesque flower hole during a televised event.

As of yet, a tour event hasn't come to SentryWorld. But that leaves more time for the rest of us to try our luck on a layout that would test the pros.

Fortunately, designer Jones gave higher handicappers a significant break. The course plays at 7,055 yards from the back tees and at 6,286 yards from the "intermediate" tees. There are also club tees measuring 5,826 yards, and forward tees at 5,197 yards.

No matter what the yardage, you'll have the experience of playing in a well-kept arboretum. In all, there are more than five acres of flowers. Birch, pine and hardwoods abound, as do hundreds of Canada geese. An extraordinary number of sprinkler heads (some 4,000 in all) help keep everything green and growing.

There's also plenty of water in hazard form. Thirty-five acres of open water became part of Jones' design, and the main lake comes into play on five holes. Lakes and creeks are lined with granite boulders blasted from bedrock during their creation, and caroms off the boulders can be helpful (sometimes) or harmful (often). Unfortunate bounces may land your ball in one of SentryWorld's 83 sand traps.

Water and sand come into prominent play on two of the back nine holes. Number 12, a 220-yard par 3, mandates a tee shot over water.

It's all carry and easy to overclub. Two oversized traps guard the green.

The 13th hole, a par 4 of 401 yards, would seem to favor a big tee shot over the huge trap at the dogleg right. But with the narrow fairway framed by water and sand, it's best to hit something less than driver to the appropriate landing area. From there, it's a full shot to a green protected by water in front, sand in back and trees to the side.

On the front nine, the 526-yard fifth hole is another great sand and water hole. Here, a narrow band of fairway horseshoes from right to left around water and a small island. Traps and trees lie along the outside perimeter of the horseshoe, requiring three good shots to get to the two-tiered green, one of many on the course.

More subtle, but just as tough, is the 511-yard par-5 ninth hole. A stream cuts diagonally across the driving area, requiring most golfers to lay up with an iron. Then it's another iron to the tree-lined dogleg. From there, it's a touchy short iron over the stream to a smallish, trapped green. Take your par gladly here.

And so it goes all around the course. Seldom, if ever, is there a shot that you don't have to think about. That didn't come about by accident. Jones, who became friends with the insurance executive, gave Joanis credit for many of the ideas that went into SentryWorld.

"We walked the ground together for five years. John is co-author," said Jones, calling Joanis a "visionary client to whom greatness without compromise was absolute."

"We did it with the soles of our feet." □

## SENTRYWORLD
601 Michigan Avenue • Stevens Point 54481 • 715/345-1600

**Directions:** Adjacent to Sentry Insurance Headquarters, north of Stevens Point
**Course:** 18 holes/par 72/7,055 yards
**Fee:** $$$$    Tee times required
**Amenities:** Pro shop; golf lessons; restaurant; club making and repair; tennis; racquetball; squash; fishing; swimming; meeting rooms; banquets

# The Springs

*The Springs' design is in definite harmony with the land, on a bend in the lower Wisconsin River.*

At a bend in the lower Wisconsin River, near the spot where Frank Lloyd Wright built Taliesin, Robert Trent Jones created one of the state's prettiest golf courses. Built some 30 years ago, the course is finally getting the attention it deserves as part of a revitalized resort complex called The Springs.

Like efforts to refurbish Taliesin, the renewed commitment to maintenance on the Jones course is heartening, although some fear the development will mean the end of a bucolic setting that has enchanted golfers for years. The new managers at The Springs vow that won't happen.

But there's no doubt that this is a busier, more hectic place than in the recent past, when the pro shop operated out of a trailer. An 80-unit hotel complex now sits alongside the 10th fairway, and low-slung condos overlook the driving range. And while the rounded, tree-topped hills from which Wright drew inspiration remain relatively unscathed, a new nine-hole course circles above the original 18.

The spectacular new nine, which is tougher and brawnier than Jones' subtle layout, was designed by Roger Packard and his partner, two-time U.S. Open champion Andy North, from nearby Madison. The new track, built across 3,300 yards of eye-catching landscape, was opened for play in 1994.

There are changes, too, in Jones' course—something that hasn't pleased golf purists. The sharp dogleg left on the 10th hole was moderated to make room for an expanded hotel pool area. The third hole was changed radically—from a subtle dogleg right to a short, straightaway hole with a very unJoneslike moat around the green. And Jones' nifty fourth hole was somewhat altered. Still, most of Jones' design remains intact. And the 6,446-yard, par-71 course is better maintained than it's been in years.

If you catch The Springs on one of those bluebird spring mornings, none of the added development or course changes will matter much. Back in the neck of the valley where the difficult 13th and 14th holes lie, the dew will be heavy upon the grass. If you're one of the first golfers through, you may glimpse a deer or turkey picking through

*Great Golf in Wisconsin*

the high grass behind the 14th tee. Whenever you arrive, you're sure to spot hawks circling above the valley.

"It's a wonderful course to play at 5:30 in the morning, when all you hear are the birds," said Robert Graves, a former Wright associate who managed the golf property until the late 1980s.

"It is unquestionably a beautiful place for a golf course," Graves said. "[Jones] had everything to work with. It couldn't be more unobtrusive than it is. It's something Mr. Wright could have understood very well."

Like Wright's prairie-style architecture, Jones' design is in harmony with the land. "I took advantage of the terrain and built a golf course," Jones said matter-of-factly years ago. "It had nothing to do with Frank Lloyd Wright." However, Jones conceded "the association was unique."

The 18th—a long par 4 that's one of Wisconsin's great finishing holes—is the highlight of Jones' masterpiece. The tee is perched midway up a hillside, where you can see the narrow, sloping landing area, with water on the right and trees on the left. The second shot is a long iron or fairway wood over water to an undulating double green that serves both the ninth and 18th holes.

When Jones designed the course, with the help of his designer son Rees, he worked without detailed drawings. Father and son simply walked the land, made rough sketches, and decided what should go where. Little earth was moved and little brush cleared. The result was a course that fit nicely into a peaceful valley set back from the big river. The valley, appropriately, is named Jones Valley (after Wright's uncle, James Lloyd Jones).

In contrast to its quiet setting, the course has not led a tranquil life. The development has had repeated spurts and stops under several owners since its beginnings under former Johnson Wax executive Willard "Bud" Keland in the mid-1960s. The golf course, while operated on a shoestring budget, managed to survive in good shape thanks to Graves' management.

For years, area golfers could decide to play on a whim, drive to Spring Green, and pay bargain-basement rates to play a Robert Trent Jones golf course. That doesn't happen anymore. Green fees are higher and tee time reservations are highly recommended. But play on the course isn't at the high-volume level yet, so an old-fashioned, four-hour round is still a possibility.

Time has brought improvements, as well. Golfers now have a place to put up their spikes and sip a beverage after a round. There's a bonafide locker room, too, in the house Euroactividade built. Euroactividade AG is the European company that stirred the valley when it announced in 1988 that it would develop a luxury resort next to Jones' course. The company sank millions into the project, which was stopped short of completion when financial problems arose.

Enter Clyde Engle and Rusty Sisson, two Chicago-area businessmen who led the cash-rich group that bought the 1,800-acre development and began to carry through with the idea of a luxury resort. Their actions in 1993 brought promise for the future. Course maintenance improved greatly, the gourmet restaurant drew rave reviews for its food, and occupancy in the well-appointed, Wright-inspired hotel was climbing, thanks to packages that promoted its luxury spa and nearby American Players Theatre.

It's finally begun to look as if the resort as a whole might match the quality of its showpiece Robert Trent Jones golf course. □

## THE SPRINGS GOLF CLUB RESORT
5857 Golf Course Road • Spring Green 53588 • 608/588-7707 or 800/626-3085

**Directions:** Hwy. 14 to Hwy. 23, southeast on Co. C, then south on Golf Course Road
**Course:** 27 holes/par71/6,446 yards, par 36/3,010 yards
**Fee:** $$$
**Amenities:** Full-service resort with suites; pro shop; restaurant; fitness/aquatics center; tennis; racquetball; volleyball; croquet; trails for walking, biking, skiing

# Trappers Turn

*A peaceful oasis on the fringe of a tourist mecca, Trappers Turn contains varied topography for an interesting game.*

There aren't any giant water slides. No neon signs advertising $1.99 breakfasts. No pyramids of brightly costumed water skiers. No sign of Yogi Bear and Boo Boo.

Can this really be Wisconsin Dells?

"Maybe if they used 'Ducks' for golf carts, that would remind you of where you are," says Roger Packard, smiling. Packard and partner Andy North, the two-time U.S. Open champion from Madison, are the designers of Trappers Turn Golf Course, a pleasant oasis on the fringe of the tourist mecca along the Wisconsin River known as Wisconsin Dells.

North and Packard made good use of the varied topography at Trappers Turn. Much of the back nine is on a ridge that drops off into a canyon along the northwest corner of the property. That's where the short, dramatic 16th hole lies. It's only 140 yards from the back tee and plays even shorter because the tee is much higher than the nest of a green that sits in the canyon below. Dark forest rises up to the left, and familiar Dells rock formations line the wall on the right. Occasionally the hills are forgiving, allowing a misdirected shot to carom down onto the green. Most often, thick underbrush grabs and holds an errant drive.

The course's lowland areas begin around Mystic Lake, a 17-acre, manmade body of water that provides the challenge of the 504-yard par-5 ninth hole. The long, tough first hole (447 yards) is also part of this lowland plain.

Number 4, a 163-yard par 3, starts from an elevated tee and heads down to a green located at the southern tip of Mystic Lake. The fifth hole starts low and climbs toward the ridge. Number 10 starts high and carries down to the lowland.

The overall effect of all this ascending and descending is a course where no two holes are alike. There's a feeling of openness on some holes—those along the ridge and around the lake—while others, like 16 and 17, are cut from heavy forest. The course butts up against Interstate 90/94 on its western border, but a heavy line of trees blocks out most of the highway sounds. The holes along that side, Nos. 14 and 15, have tiered fairways that fall off left into thick woods and underbrush.

The designers took care to disturb as little of this spectacular natural terrain as possible. "You don't have to spend a zillion dollars to get a great golf course, and you don't have to go crazy to design tricks," Packard says. "Besides, Andy wouldn't let me cut down any trees."

The goal, according to North, was to design a course that was friendly, not fearsome. "You don't have brain damage out here after you get done playing," he says. "You're not going to lose 35 golf balls."

North is a veteran on the corporate golf circuit, which helps him identify with the mid- to high-handicap player. "I have come to understand that you don't need to force him to carry the ball 250 yards over caverns," he says. "All that proves is that the guy can't do it, and he knows that before he starts." So there are no monstrous carries over water or wasteland at Trappers Turn. If you're a golfer who, more often than not, plays along the ground, you can play your normal game here.

The course is short, ranging from 5,043 yards at its shortest, to only 6,360 yards from the championship tees—although future plans call for building some new tees and greens that will add length to the layout.

The challenge at Trappers Turn lies in making the right decisions. The third hole, for example, is a straight par 4 of only 273 yards. The big hitter is tempted to try to drive the green. The danger lies in woods close by the green on the left and to the rear, and a steeped-faced bunker at the front, which make a 6 as likely a score for the gambler as a 3 or a 4.

At 342 yards, the fifth hole is another short par 4, with the lake to the right and out-of-bounds to the left off the tee. The second shot is uphill to a sloping green.

North likens those holes to short par 4s on famous courses like Harbour Town in Hilton Head, South Carolina, and Cypress Point on California's Monterey Peninsula.

"I don't think there are enough holes like that being designed anymore," he says. "Cypress Point has back-to-back 300-yard par 4s, and I've made more sixes on those two holes than on any others on tour."

The par-5 ninth hole offers another risk-and-reward challenge. At 504 yards, the green can be reached in two shots but to do so requires a drive that hugs the right side—the side that runs along Mystic Lake—and a second shot that must clear the stream in front of the green. Most of us will hit short of the stream and try to make our birdie with a good wedge shot and a putt.

Perhaps the most scenic hole is No. 10. From an elevated tee, the hole bends left around a forested hillside. A brook that feeds into the lake begins at a rock waterfall near the green, crosses the fairway, and meanders down the left side towards the tee. A small, two-tiered green awaits the second shot.

The stream also comes into play on No. 18, a quirky par 5 with a sharp dropoff about 210 yards from the back tee.

Anything hit longer could bounce right or left into the trees. From the edge of the drop-off, the second shot is either a very long poke over the stream, which cuts diagonally across the fairway, or a lay-up. The green is severely sloped from right to left, so much so that most shots, regardless of where they land on the green, end up somewhere along the left edge.

Plans call for a new green to be built behind the existing green and reshaping the entire fairway to present a slope that's more gradual.

Trappers Turn opened in 1991, nearly a year behind schedule. The original developers ran into financial difficulty when a condominium project on the property failed to produce enough revenue to pay for completion of the course.

Eventually the project was sold to Bob and Patricia Francis of Green Lake. Under their direction, the course was completed and a beautiful clubhouse was built in timely fashion.

Trappers Turn is now working on building a reputation as one of the finest golf courses in the state. In North's view, the course will be successful if the people who play it have fun and want to return.

"Neither Roger nor I have egos such that we're going to be building monuments to ourselves," he says. "I like to create really nice courses that people get a lot of joy out of playing. To me, that's reward enough."

It's not Storybook Gardens or the wax museum, but Trappers Turn has definitely become one of the attractions not to be missed at Wisconsin Dells. □

## TRAPPERS TURN GOLF COURSE
P.O. Box 176 • Wisconsin Dells 53965 • 608/253-7000

**Directions:** I-90/94, exit 85, turn east on Hwy. 12/16,
   then 1 1/2 miles to course
**Course:** 18 holes/par 72/6,051 yards
**Fee:** $$$ (Fee includes cart)   Tee times required;
   carts required until 3 p.m.
**Amenities:** Clubhouse; dining room; bar and grill;
   scenic veranda with view; pro shop; locker rooms

# University Ridge

*Good length. Much diversity. Subtle challenges.
Lots of gorgeous Wisconsin landscape.*

Most golfers who play University Ridge have no idea of how long it took the University of Wisconsin to get this course built.

They are aware, however, that the university did it right, no matter how long it took. There are four or five tee areas on every hole—most are elevated, so the course plays 5,005 yards at its shortest distance and 6,825 yards from the back tee, with progressive challenges in between.

Number 10, a par 4 stretching 456 yards off the back tee, is certainly one of the best holes on this Robert Trent Jones II layout, which was rated as one of the top new public courses of 1992 by *Golf Digest* magazine. The fairway is slightly pitched from right to left. Since the entire back nine is cut from dense woods, trees on both sides are an ever-present danger.

Even a great drive leaves a long-iron shot to an elongated, two-tiered green that's guarded on the left by a bunker as long as the green. It's tempting to bail out to the right, but the ground rises from the green toward the next tee, so if the ball gets hung up on the hill, it's nearly impossible to get up and down for par. A great hole.

And so it goes at University Ridge, which is located in the town of Verona, just south and west of Madison. Good length. Much diversity. Subtle challenges. Lots of gorgeous Wisconsin landscape. The wooded back nine is hilly and secluded; the front nine rolls gently over former farmlands.

Bruce Charlton, the lead designer for the Jones company, said he and Jones immediately fell in love with what they saw in the raw landscape. "We liked the natural topography, the way it rolled and folded and moved uphill and downhill," Charlton said. "It was a golf architect's dream to lay out something on that kind of property."

No two holes are alike. The par-5 sixth hole, for example, is 608 yards long, with a tiered green that falls off sharply to the left. Two large traps, one set into the left bank, guard the opening.

By contrast, No. 15 is a downhill par 4 of only 343 yards from the back tee, but it's tricky because the drive must be played away from trees on the right and short of two big sand traps that lie at the corner of the dogleg on the left. Use something less than a driver off the tee, then a short iron off a sloping lie to the narrow green. Tall trees near the hole on the right side prevent any percentage chance of cutting the corner and staying out of trouble.

Jones is proud of his work at University Ridge. Although it's young, Jones said the course compares favorably with the best university courses in the country, including world-renowned layouts at Yale, Stanford and Ohio State. "The course is very free," Jones said. "It's truly a golf course. It's not a housing development or a resort. It's a classic golf course, spread out over the acreage of the property in a very generous way."

Speaking of generosity, it was donations by UW alums Harry Culver and Carl Dietze that made it possible for the university to consider building a golf course...and consider it...and consider it.

Culver, a Chicago physician, died unexpectedly in 1965 while on a golf vacation in Scotland. He left nearly $1 million to the UW Foundation, to be used for sports and recreational purposes.

Dietze, a Milwaukee attorney and accountant who died in 1970, bequeathed nearly $1 million to the foundation to be used to build a golf course. The foundation sat on this nest egg for years while it entertained proposals for a course at various sites in and around Madison. While the current property was purchased in the 1970s, it was 1986 before the university gave the final go-ahead on the project.

In 1991, the $5.5 million course called University Ridge finally opened.

Today we can look past the history of false starts to a landscape of bright-green bentgrass fairways and greens, outlined by darker blue-grass roughs and framed by cherry, oak and maple trees.

Did we mention the signature hole? It has to be No. 16, a par 5 of 533 yards from the back tee that features two fairways and a cluster of bunkers (a dozen, count 'em), right where a decent second shot should land.

The safe and sane route is to the left—straight off the tee, with a straight second shot to where the fairway turns right (keep to the left of the traps), then a short chip shot to a big green.

The foolhardy will try the path to the right. The tee shot must find the opening in the trees to the right (big trees, small opening) to reach a safe landing area. There's almost no margin for error since anything that drifts even a little bit right will land in dense rough.

Okay, so maybe there's a chance to reach the green in two after a miracle tee shot. It's still not worth the risk.

The toughest hole on the course, especially from the back tee, might be No. 4. The hole is 444 yards uphill, with the marshy fringe of Morse Pond to the right off the tee.

The long second shot must find the opening between trees that pinch the fairway about 70 yards in front of the greatly elevated green and the steep bank sloping to the pond. Even from the second-longest tee, a full 90 yards shorter, this hole is no picnic.

The final two holes make for an interesting finish. Number 17, a par 3 of 199 yards from the back tee, is mostly downhill over a pond that creeps up nearly to the green. The 18th is a hike—a 413-yard dogleg left, uphill all the way, with bunkers down the left side to discourage attempting a shortcut.

University Ridge is home to the UW men's and women's golf teams and would someday be an ideal host for the National Collegiate Athletic Association Championships—a goal the university is already pursuing.

The O.J. Noer Center for Turfgrass Research is located on the property, adjacent to the golf course. Long-range plans call for construction of another 18-hole course, plus a state-of-the-art learning center. But they'll have to wait until funds are available.

In the meantime, the University of Wisconsin has what it's been seeking since the Eisenhower era—a golf course of which it can be proud. □

## UNIVERSITY RIDGE GOLF COURSE
7120 County Trunk PD • Verona 53593 • 608/845-7700

**Directions:** From Mineral Point Road, Co. M
   south to Co. PD, then west one-half mile
**Course:** 18 holes/par 72/6,825 yards
**Fee:** $$$$    Carts required on weekends
**Amenities:** Driving range; golf shop; refreshment area;
   putting greens

# Northwest Courses

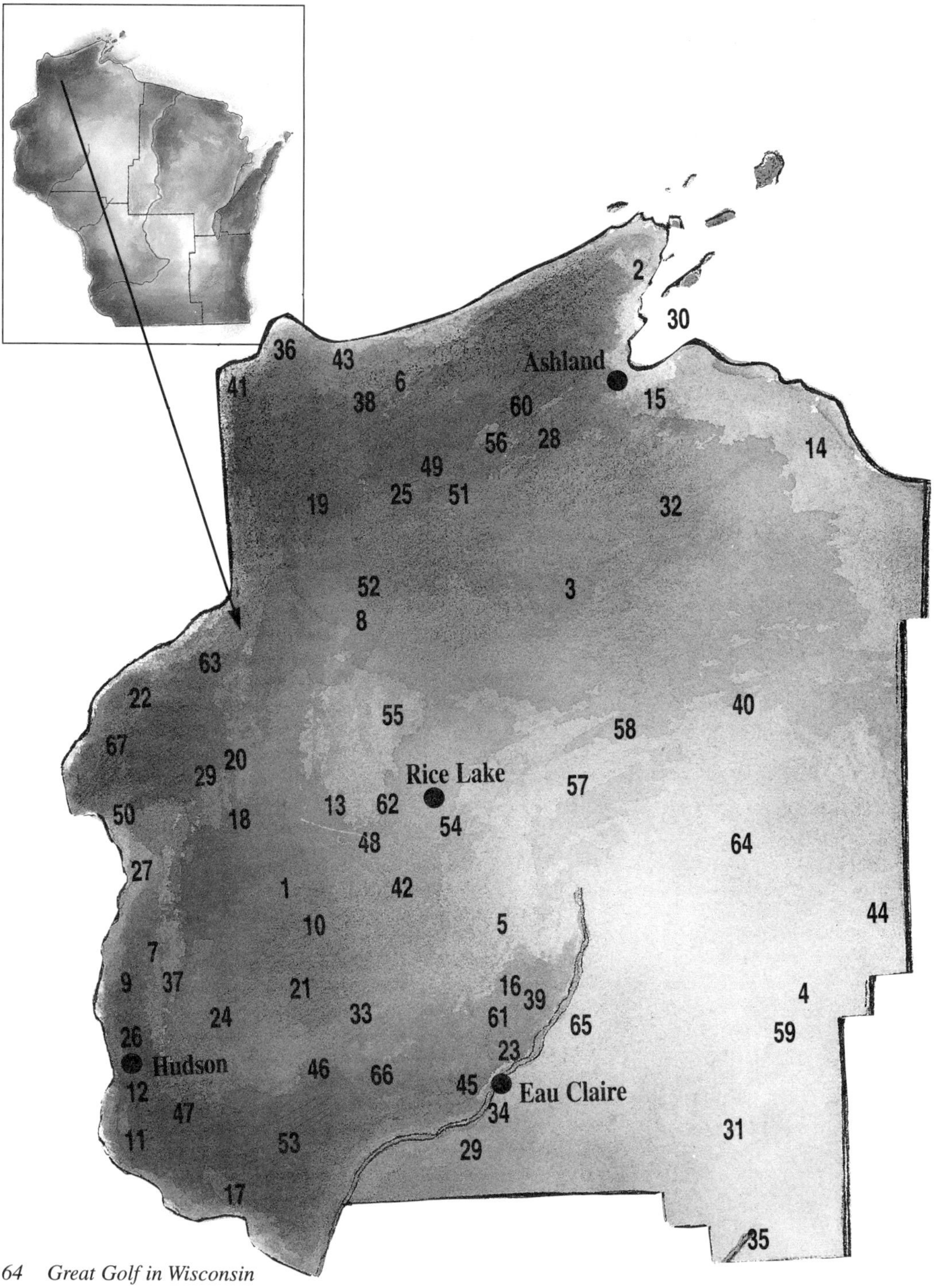

# Northwest

| No. | Page |
|---|---|
| 1 AMERY GOLF COURSE | 66 |
| 2 APOSTLE HIGHLANDS | 66 |
| 3 BARKER LAKE COUNTRY LODGE & GC | 66 |
| 4 BLACK RIVER COUNTRY CLUB | 66 |
| 5 BLOOMER MEMORIAL GOLF COURSE | 67 |
| 6 BOTTEN'S GREEN ACRES GOLF COURSE | 67 |
| 7 BRISTOL RIDGE GOLF COURSE | 67 |
| 8 BUTTERNUT HILLS GOLF COURSE | 68 |
| 9 CHABRE GOLF COURSE | 68 |
| 10 CLEAR LAKE GOLF COURSE | 68 |
| 11 CLIFTON HIGHLANDS GOLF COURSE | 68 |
| 12 CLIFTON HOLLOW GOLF COURSE | 69 |
| 13 CUMBERLAND GOLF COURSE | 69 |
| 14 EAGLE BLUFF GOLF COURSE | 69 |
| 15 ELKS COUNTRY CLUB, ASHLAND | 69 |
| 16 ELKS COUNTRY CLUB, CHIPPEWA FALLS | 70 |
| 17 ELLSWORTH COUNTRY CLUB | 70 |
| 18 FIVE FLAGS COUNTRY CLUB | 70 |
| 19 FOREST POINT GOLF COURSE | 70 |
| 20 FREDERIC COUNTRY CLUB | 70 |
| 21 GLEN HILLS GOLF COURSE | 70 |
| 22 GRANTSBURG MUNICIPAL GOLF COURSE | 71 |
| 23 HALLIE GOLF COURSE | 71 |
| 24 HAMMOND GOLF COURSE | 71 |
| 25 HAYWARD GOLF & TENNIS CLUB | 72 |
| 26 HUDSON COUNTRY CLUB | 72 |
| 27 KROOKED KREEK GOLF COURSE | 72 |
| 28 LAKEWOODS FOREST RIDGES GOLF COURSE | 72 |
| 29 LUCK GOLF COURSE | 72 |
| 30 MADELINE ISLAND GOLF COURSE | 73 |
| 31 MEADOWVIEW GOLF COURSE | 73 |
| 32 MELLEN COUNTRY CLUB | 73 |
| 33 MENOMONIE GOLF & COUNTRY CLUB | 74 |
| 34 MILL RUN GOLF COURSE | 74 |
| 35 NEILLSVILLE GOLF COURSE | 74 |
| 36 NEMADJI GOLF COURSE | 74 |
| 37 NEW RICHMOND GOLF COURSE | 75 |
| 38 NORWOOD GOLF COURSE | 75 |
| 39 OJIBWA GOLF AND BOWL | 75 |
| 40 PARK FALLS GOLF COURSE | 76 |
| 41 PATTISON PARK GOLF COURSE | 76 |
| 42 PINE CREST GOLF | 76 |
| 43 POPLAR GOLF & RECREATION AREA | 76 |
| 44 PRENTICE VILLAGE GOLF COURSE | 76 |
| 45 PRINCETON VALLEY GOLF COURSE | 76 |
| 46 RAINBOW RIDGE GOLF COURSE | 77 |
| 47 RIVER FALLS GOLF COURSE | 77 |
| 48 ROLLING OAKS GOLF COURSE | 77 |
| 49 ROYNONA CREEK GOLF COURSE | 78 |
| 50 ST. CROIX VALLEY COUNTRY CLUB | 78 |
| 51 SPIDER LAKE COUNTRY CLUB | 78 |
| 52 SPOONER GOLF COURSE | 78 |
| 53 SPRING VALLEY GOLF COURSE | 78 |
| 54 SUNSET VIEW COUNTRY CLUB | 79 |
| 55 TAGALONG GOLF COURSE | 79 |
| 56 TAHKODAH HILLS GOLF COURSE | 79 |
| 57 TAYLOR'S AMACOY GOLF & SUPPER CLUB | 80 |
| 58 TEE-A-WAY GOLF & SUPPER CLUB | 80 |
| 59 TEE-HI CLUB | 80 |
| 60 TELEMARK GOLF COURSE | 80 |
| 61 TIMBER TERRACE GOLF COURSE | 80 |
| 62 TURTLEBACK GOLF & COUNTRY CLUB | 81 |
| 63 VOYAGER VILLAGE COUNTRY CLUB | 81 |
| 64 WESTWOOD GOLF & SUPPER CLUB | 82 |
| 65 WHISPERING PINES GOLF COURSE | 82 |
| 66 WHITETAIL GOLF COURSE | 83 |
| 67 YELLOW LAKE GOLF COURSE | 83 |

## AMERY GC

601 Deronda Rd. • Amery 54001 • 715/268-7213

**Directions:** One-half mile west of Hwy. 46 on Co. F
**Course:** 18 holes/par 71/6,340 yards
**Fee:** $$
**Amenities:** Pro shop; bar; banquet facilities; grill; driving range; practice facility

Eleven of the 18 holes have water. This scenic course has abundant wildlife.

## APOSTLE HIGHLANDS

1433 Apostle Highlands Blvd. • P. O. Box 850 • Bayfield 54814 • 715/779-5960

**Directions:** One mile south of Bayfield via Hwy. 13 and Co. J
**Course:** 9 holes/par 36/3,249 yards
**Fee:** $$   Tee times required, carts may be required on weekends

Located on the bluffs over Bayfield, the course offers spectacular views of Lake Superior and its Apostle Islands. A back nine is under construction with a completion date of fall 1994.

## BARKER LAKE COUNTRY LODGE & GC

W6841 Golf Course Rd. • Winter 54896 • 715/266-7361 or 715/266-4152

**Directions:** Co. W north out of Winter to Co. B east, then follow signs 25 miles east out of Hayward
**Course:** 9 holes/par 35/2,796 yards
**Fee:** $

Thought to be opened in the 1920s, this course recently has begun to see improvements, including sand traps and larger greens.

## BLACK RIVER CC

W5291 Co. O • Medford 54451 • 715/748-5520

**Directions:** On the south side of Medford, go east on Co. O about one mile
**Course:** 9 holes/par 35/2,958 yards
**Fee:** $   Tee times required

This new course, opened in 1992, promotes its greens as some of the most challenging in the state. The course is well-bunkered (21 sand traps in all) and has water hazards on four holes.

# BLOOMER MEMORIAL GC

500 13th Ave. • Bloomer 54724 • 715/568-1741

**Directions:** Four blocks east of Main Street on 13th Avenue
**Course:** 9 holes/par 35/2,870 yards
**Fee:** $
**Amenities:** Pro shop; bar

Landscaping and an irrigation system already have improved the older nine's appearance. The terrain has just enough gentle roll to give the course character. Thousands of mature pines and a few well-placed maples give it a nice northwoods feel. This course tests golfers with nine greenside traps and two water hazards, which come into play on two different holes.

# BOTTEN'S GREEN ACRES GC

7171 S. Co. S • Lake Nebagamon 54849 • 715/374-2567

**Directions:** One mile south of Lake Nebagamon
**Course:** 9 holes/par 35/2,830 yards
**Fee:** $
**Amenities:** Driving range

# BRISTOL RIDGE GC

1978 Co. C • Somerset 54025 • 715/247-5538

**Directions:** Hwy. 64 to Co. C, north two miles along the Apple River
**Course:** 18 holes/par 72/6,600 yards
**Fees:** Unavailable at time of printing
**Amenities:** Pro shop; clubhouse; bar and grill

This fully irrigated championship course, opening in July 1994, features multiple water hazards and mature hardwoods and pines.

*New Richmond Golf Course*

*Sorry, no hunting.* Deer roam the fairways of Telemark Country Club in Cable.

## BUTTERNUT HILLS GC

HCR 69 • Box 131 • Sarona 54870 • 715/635-8563

**Directions:** Hwy. 53 to Co. B, about 18 miles north of Rice Lake, six miles east on B
**Course:** 18 holes/par 70/5,625 yards
**Fee:** $   Tee times required

The second nine of this relatively new course is still being improved. The first nine was built in 1978; the second in 1993. Both have beautiful bluegrass fairways set on rolling terrain characterized by big trees. Sand traps are on the older nine only.

## CHABRE GC

407 Hwy. 64 • Somerset 54025 • 715/247-5506

**Directions:** Six miles from Stillwater on Hwy. 64
**Course:** 9 holes/par 33/2,750 yards
**Fee:** $
**Amenities:** Driving range, practice green

## CLEAR LAKE GC

250 Golf Dr. • P. O. Box 283 • Clear Lake 54005 • 715/263-2500

**Directions:** North on Hwy. 63, to fifth Clear Lake exit, 1/2 mile on right
**Course:** 9 holes/par 36/3,014 yards
**Fee:** $
**Amenities:** Driving range; bar; pro shop

This course sports wide fairways, some hills, water on two holes and trees to test you.

## CLIFTON HIGHLANDS GC

N6890 1230th St. • Prescott 54021 • 715/262-5141 or 800/657-6845

**Directions:** Two miles northeast of Prescott on Co. MM and Co. F, 30 miles from downtown St. Paul, two miles from St. Croix and Mississippi rivers
**Course:** 18 holes/par 72/6,619 yards
**Fee:** $$   Tee times required 7 days in advance
**Amenities:** New clubhouse; full pro shop; bar & grill; driving range; PGA pro available

Beautiful championship golf course in the scenic St. Croix River Valley.

## CLIFTON HOLLOW GC

W12166 820th Ave. • River Falls 54022 •
715/425-9781 or 800/487-8879

**Directions:** Eight miles south of Hudson on Co. F
**Course:** 27 holes/par 72/6,381 yards, par 27/1,076 yards
**Fee:** $$   Tee times required
**Amenities:** Clubhouse; nine-hole par-3 course

Close to the scenic St. Croix River and picturesque Kinnickinnic State Park, this course features rolling terrain, sloping greens, bluegrass fairways, bentgrass greens and hundreds of trees, new and old. One memorable hole on the decade-old course: the 635-yard, par-5 ninth hole. A new clubhouse was added in 1987. The nine-hole par-3 course, added in 1985, features what the course managers describe as a "110-yard putting hole."

## CUMBERLAND GC

2501 5th St. • Cumberland 54829 • 715/822-4333

**Directions:** West of Cumberland on Hwy. 48
**Course:** 18 holes/par 72/6,242 yards
**Fee:** $$
**Amenities:** Driving range; small banquet facilities; clubhouse

Narrow fairways and abundant water make this course challenging to play.

## EAGLE BLUFF GC

Co. D • P.O. Box 265 • Hurley 54534 • 715/561-3552

**Directions:** West of Hurley off Hwy. 2 on Co. D
**Course:** 18 holes/par 69/5,842 yards
**Fee:** $   Tee times required on weekends
**Amenities:** Clubhouse serving cocktails, sandwiches and pizza

This northwoods golf outpost, built in 1967, is advertised as a hilly and scenic track that is especially pretty in the fall.

## ELKS CC

Hwy. 137 • P.O. Box 364 • Ashland 54806 • 715/682-5215

**Directions:** Main Street to Sanborn Avenue, south on Sanborn to Hwy. 137, then west on 137 for one mile
**Course:** 9 holes/par 36/3,150 yards
**Fee:** $$

This course, dating back to 1930, provides great views of Chequamegon Bay and Lake Superior's Apostle Islands.

*Great Golf in Wisconsin*

## ELKS CC

Route 5 • P. O. Box 764 • Chippewa Falls 54729 • 715/723-7363

**Directions:** Hwy. 124 through Chippewa Falls to Co. S, then east one-quarter mile
**Course:** 9 holes/par 35/2,897 yards
**Fee:** $

## ELLSWORTH CC

Hwy. 65 North, Golf Course Lane • Ellsworth 54011 • 715/273-4438

**Directions:** 1 1/2 miles north of Ellsworth on Hwy. 65
**Course:** 9 holes/par 36/3,111 yards
**Fee:** $$    Tee times required on weekends from 8 a.m. to 4 p.m.

Built in 1963, this course is for the average player. Rolling terrain, many pine trees and watered bluegrass fairways make for nice surroundings.

## FIVE FLAGS CC

Route 2 • P. O. Box 312 • Balsam Lake 54810 • 715/825-2141

**Directions:** Polk County near Balsam Lake
**Course:** 9 holes/par 36/3,136 yards
**Fee:** $
**Amenities:** Pro shop; bar

Rolling hills and water hazards characterize this course.

## FOREST POINT GC

Route 1 • P. O. Box 156 • Gordon 54838 • 715/376-2322

**Directions:** Fourteen miles east of Gordon off Co. Y
**Course:** 9 holes/par 33/2,284 yards
**Fee:** $

This course, built in 1932, now features a pond and waterfall on the No. 1 fairway.

## FREDERIC CC

South Hwy. 35 • P. O. Box 219 • Frederic 54837 • 715/327-8250

**Directions:** One mile south of Frederic on Hwy. 35
**Course:** 9 holes/par 35/2,920 yards
**Fee:** $$
**Amenities:** Driving range; pro shop; bar; practice green

## GLEN HILLS GC

P. O. Box 247 • Glenwood City 54013 • 715/265-4718

**Directions:** I-94 to Hwy. 128 north, east on Co. E one mile, then left on Rustic Road 3 to Campground Lane
**Course:** 9 holes/par 36/3,377 yards
**Fee:** $    Tee times required
**Amenities:** Pro shop; restaurant; driving range; Glen Hills Park available for camping, swimming, fishing & hiking

## GRANTSBURG MUNICIPAL GC

333 W. St. George Ave. • Grantsburg 54840 • 715/463-2300

**Directions:** Hwy. 70 to intersection of Hwy. 48/87, one block north on Pine Street, then west on St. George Avenue
**Course:** 9 holes/par 33/2,215 yards
**Fee:** $

This short nine-hole layout was built in 1966. It has rolling terrain, bentgrass greens, bluegrass, tree-lined fairways and an automatic watering system.

## HALLIE GC

3798 Golfview Dr. • Chippewa Falls 54729 • 715/723-8524

**Directions:** I-94 to Eau Claire, exit on Hwy. 53 north, then through Eau Claire to Co. J
**Course:** 18 holes/par 70/5,787 yards
**Fee:** $$
**Amenities:** Pro shop; restaurant & bar; driving range; custom outings

This course has tree-lined fairways and multiple water hazards.

## HAMMOND GC

450 Davis St. • P.O. Box 236 • Hammond 54015 • 715/796-2266

**Directions:** I-94 to Hammond exit, 2 1/2 miles north of I-94, 35 miles east of St. Paul
**Course:** 9 holes/par 36/3,088 yards
**Fee:** $$    Tee times required, nonmember tee times can be scheduled 48 hours in advance
**Amenities:** Driving range; full irrigation; elevated greens

More than 1,000 trees have been planted on this course, which features water on four holes, 18 greenside sand traps and a long par 5 at the 580-yard fourth hole.

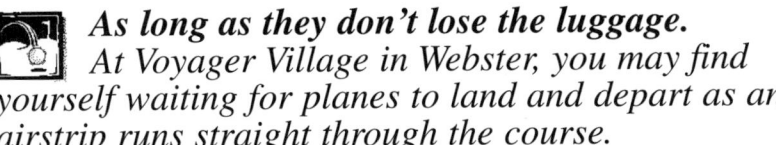

*As long as they don't lose the luggage. At Voyager Village in Webster, you may find yourself waiting for planes to land and depart as an airstrip runs straight through the course.*

## HAYWARD GOLF & TENNIS CLUB

Route 10 Box 543 • Wittwer Street • Hayward 54843 • 715/634-2760

**Directions:** One-half mile north of downtown Hayward on Wittwer Street
**Course:** 18 holes/par 72/6,597 yards
**Fee:** $$

## HUDSON CC

378 Frontage Rd. • Hudson 54016 • 715/386-3390

**Directions:** Seventeen miles east of St. Paul, I-94 on the Wisconsin/Minnesota border
**Course:** 18 holes/par 71/6,405 yards
**Fee:** $$     Tee times required
**Amenities:** Pro shop; driving range; food & beverages; PGA pro

Rolling hills, well-manicured greens combined with interesting par 3s provide a challenge to all skill levels.

## KROOKED KREEK GC

2448 75th Ave., Co. M • Osceola 54020 • 715/755-3673 or 715/294-3673

**Directions:** One mile east of Osceola on Co. M
**Course:** 9 holes/par 36/3,160 yards
**Fee:** $

## LAKEWOODS FOREST RIDGES GC

HC73 • Box 715 • Cable 54821 • 715/794-2561 or 800/255-5937

**Directions:** Eight miles east of Cable on Co. M
**Course:** 18 holes/par 71/6,270 yards
**Fee:** $$
**Amenities:** Teaching center; driving range; complete pro shop; bar and grill serving all meals; motel units, condos and cottages on Lake Namakagon; full-service marina; tennis courts; indoor/outdoor pools and whirlpool

This course is opening its back nine in July 1994 and the remaining nine in September.

## LUCK GC

1520 S. Shore Dr. • Luck 54853 • 715/472-2939

**Directions:** East of Hwy. 35 on the south shore of Big Butternut Lake
**Course:** 18 holes/par 71/6,122 yards
**Fee:** $$     Tee times required

**Amenities:** Driving range; camping; pro shop; snack bar

This course features a lot of water, trees and nice views. The original nine holes were built in the late 1930s; the course went to 18 holes in the late 1980s. Water can be found on seven holes, but you'd have to hit it wild to land in Big Butternut Lake, across the entry road.

## MADELINE ISLAND GC

P. O. Box 83 • La Pointe 54850 • 715/747-3212

**Directions:** North of Ashland on Hwy. 13, 15-minute ferry ride from Bayfield
**Course:** 18 holes/par 71/6,366 yards
**Fee:** $$$   Carts required (not included in fee)
**Amenities:** Pro shop; driving range; putting green; snack bar

Designed by Robert Trent Jones, this course has large, shared double greens, which are approached by distinctly different fairways.

## MEADOWVIEW GC

800 W. Third St. • P. O. Box 327 • Owen 54460 • 715/229-2355

**Directions:** One-quarter mile north of Hwy. 29 on Co. X in Owen
**Course:** 9 holes/par 36/3,172 yards
**Fee:** $
**Amenities:** Large banquet facilities; pro shop; restaurant

This northwoods course, built in 1926, has several challenging holes, particularly the back five.

## MELLEN CC

Mellen 54546 • 715/274-7311

**Directions:** North of Mellen on Co. C
**Course:** 9 holes/par 34/2,979 yards
**Fee:** $

This old course (built in 1926) isn't fancy, but its hilly terrain and forested surroundings make for a nice outing while in the northwoods.

*Yellow Lake Golf Course in Danbury*

## MENOMONIE G & CC

802 Heller Rd. • Menomonie 54751 • 715/235-3595

**Directions:** Hwy. 25 (Broadway) to Pine Avenue, then left on Heller Road
**Course:** 9 holes/par 30/1,810 yards
**Fee:** $   Tee times required

A new clubhouse and additional water hazards are planned for 1994.

## MILL RUN GC

3905 Kane Rd. • Eau Claire 54703 • 715/834-1766 or 800/260-3000

**Directions:** I-94 to exit 59, east on Hwy 12 to Eau Claire for 1 1/2 miles to Kane Road, then south on Kane one-half mile
**Course:** 18 holes/par 70/6,064 yards
**Fee:** $$
**Amenities:** Driving range and practice green-trap; locker room facilities; lounge and patio serving light lunches

This relatively new course (all of it built during the 1980s) is known for its fine landscaping, especially the many flowers that decorate the gently rolling terrain. The course is fairly open, but water hazards compensate for that. Water can come into play on 11 holes. Sand traps and a big waste sand area add to the challenge.

## NEILLSVILLE GC

603 E. Division St. • Neillsville 54456 • 715/743-3780

**Directions:** On Hwy. 10, east of Hwy. 73
**Course:** 9 holes/par 36/3,055 yards
**Fee:** $
**Amenities:** Restaurant; bar; Friday fish fry

This rolling course, located in the center of the state, is for all levels.

## NEMADJI GC

5 N. 58th St. East • Superior 54880 • 715/394-9022

**Directions:** Three miles west of Hwy. 2
**Course:** 36 holes/par 71/6,337 yards, par 72/6,683 yards
**Fee:** $$   Tee times required
**Amenities:** Clubhouse serving food and drinks; pro shop; driving range

A nine-hole layout, added in 1991, that cuts through deep woods and ravines makes a visit to this course worthwhile. The original 18 (built in 1932) is flat. But the new nine and one built in 1984 provide a more modern, tougher challenge that includes water. This is one of the finest public courses in the Twin Ports area.

## NEW RICHMOND GC

1226 180th Ave. • New Richmond 54017 • 715/246-6724

**Directions:** One-half mile west of New Richmond on Hwy. 64
**Course:** 18 holes/par 72/6,716 yards
**Fee:** $$$
**Amenities:** Pro shop; grill; driving range

With a slope rating of 136 from the blue tees, New Richmond will challenge your golfing skills. Mature trees and well-trapped greens set on 175 acres of beautiful rolling terrain assure you of a memorable golf experience.

## NORWOOD GC

7445 S. Co. P • Lake Nebagamon 54849 • 715/374-3210

**Directions:** One mile north of Lake Minnesuing on Co. P,
20 miles south of Superior
**Course:** 9 holes/par 31/2,015 yards
**Fee:** $     Tee times required on weekends
**Amenities:** Pro shop; food & beverages

This hilly course provides a challenging round of nine.

## OJIBWA GOLF AND BOWL

Hwy. 124 North, Route 5 • Chippewa Falls 54729 • 715/723-8823

**Directions:** One mile north of Leinenkugel Brewery
**Course:** 9 holes/par 34/2,852 yards
**Fee:** $

This mature course (1920s vintage) boasts of a friendly atmosphere, many trees, a scenic pond and an unusual island tee area on one par 3. There are no par 5s but a few long par 4s to test your skill.

*Forest Point Golf Course in Gordon*

## PARK FALLS GC

Saunders Avenue • Park Falls 54552 • 715/762-4396

**Directions:** East of Hwy. 13, one mile north of Hwy. 182
**Course:** 9 holes/par 35/2,946 yards
**Fee:** $$
**Amenities:** Bar; limited pro shop

## PATTISON PARK GC

Route 2 • 4111 E. Co. B • Superior 54880-8332 • 715/399-2489

**Directions:** East of Hwy. 35 on Co. B (about 3 miles)
**Course:** 9 holes/par 31/2,035 yards
**Fee:** $

## PINE CREST GOLF

P. O. Box 44 • Dallas 54733 • 715/837-1268

**Directions:** One-half mile north of Dallas on Co. U
**Course:** 9 holes/par 35/2,741 yards
**Fee:** $

## POPLAR GOLF & RECREATION AREA

Route 1 • P. O. Box 796 • Poplar 54864 • 715/364-2689

**Directions:** About 13 miles east of Superior on Hwy. 2, then north on Co. D about 1 1/2 miles from Poplar
**Course:** 9 holes/par 31/3,300 yards
**Fee:** $

Nine new holes are under construction at this out-of-the-way course. The current nine, built in 1961, is a beautiful wooded layout featuring a river that comes into play on four of the holes.

## PRENTICE VILLAGE GC

403 Center St. • Prentice 54556 • 715/428-2127

**Directions:** East of Hwy. 13 on Co. A
**Course:** 9 holes/par 34/2,353 yards
**Fee:** $

## PRINCETON VALLEY GC

2300 W. Princeton Ave. • Eau Claire 54703 • 715/834-3334

**Directions:** Take Hwy. 53 to North Crossing, east to LaSalle Street, then left 2 miles to Gooder
**Course:** 9 holes/par 36/3,025 yards

**Fee:** $   Tee times required
**Amenities:** Lighted driving range with PGA pro

This course, built in 1976, is in a suburban setting and has watered bluegrass fairways and rough. The course is characterized by its big bentgrass greens.

## RAINBOW RIDGE GC

2200 Crestwood Dr. • Menomonie 54751 • 715/235-9808

**Directions:** I-94 to Menomonie exit, south on Hwy. 25 (Broadway) to 21st Avenue, left on 21st Avenue, then right on 9th Street and left on 490th Avenue
**Course:** 9 holes/par 36/3,250 yards
**Fee:** $
**Amenities:** Driving range; lounge serving drinks and snacks

Built in 1976, this well-groomed course is situated on gently rolling terrain that features a variety of trees including oak, maple, birch, cherry and pine. Tree-lined fairways provide a very scenic layout. Water comes into play on two holes.

## RIVER FALLS GC

1011 Co. M East • River Falls 54022 • 715/425-7253

**Directions:** Ten miles south of I-94, 1 1/2 miles east on Co. M off bypass
**Course:** 18 holes/par 72/6,471 yards
**Fee:** $$

## ROLLING OAKS GC

440 W. Division • Barron 54812 • 715/537-3409

**Directions:** West end of Barron on Hwy. 8
**Course:** 9 holes/par 35/2,882 yards
**Fee:** $   Tee times required on weekends
**Amenities:** Food & beverages; putting green; pro shop

This scenic course has numerous oak trees.

*True grit.* Sand greens–some of the few remaining in the country–are the highlight of the Yellow Lake Golf Club, between Webster and Danbury. You can play there summer and winter (provided you can swing in your snowmobile suit). Special snow balls and, for night play, glow-in-the-dark balls are available.

## ROYNONA CREEK GC

Hwy. 63 North • Route 10, Box 1 • Hayward 54843 • 715/634-5880

**Directions:** One-quarter of a mile north of Hayward on Hwy. 63
**Course:** 9 holes/par 30/1,675 yards
**Fee:** $
**Amenities:** Clubhouse; snack bar; rentals

This course has plenty of water hazards to challenge golfers in all levels of play.

## ST. CROIX VALLEY CC

Hwy. 8 • St. Croix Falls 54024 • 715/483-3377

**Directions:** 1 1/2 miles east of St. Croix
**Course:** 9 holes/par 35/2,797 yards
**Fee:** $

## SPIDER LAKE CC

Route 1, Murphy Blvd. • Hayward 54843 • 715/462-3200

**Directions:** Thirteen miles east of Hayward on Hwy. 77 to Murphy Boulevard, north about two miles
**Course:** 9 holes/par 36/3,200 yards
**Fee:** $$
**Amenities:** Full bar serving sandwiches

This revamped course promotes its landscaping and conditioning. It boasts new sand traps and a log shelter for 1994.

## SPOONER GC

Co. H • Spooner 54801 • 715/635-3580

**Directions:** 2 1/2 miles from Spooner on Hwy. 53, northeast on Co. H
**Course:** 18 holes/par 71/6,407 yards
**Fee:** $$
**Amenities:** Pro shop; locker room; restaurant; driving range

## SPRING VALLEY GC

Van Buren Road • P. O. Box 8 • Spring Valley 54767 • 715/778-5513

**Directions:** Two miles west of Spring Valley on Hwy. 29, one-half mile north on Van Buren Road
**Course:** 18 holes/par 71/6,104 yards
**Fee:** $$

Nine new holes were added to this course in 1987.

## SUNSET VIEW CC

1013 Sunset View Rd. • Chetek 54728 • 715/859-6211

**Directions:** Three miles north of Chetek on Co. M
**Course:** 9 holes/par 34/2,240 yards
**Fee:** $    Tee times required on weekends only
**Amenities:** Driving range

This course, built in 1925, is short but tricky. Pokegama Lake comes into play on two holes.

## TAGALONG GC

P. O. Box 68 • Birchwood 54817 • 715/354-3458

**Directions:** One mile south of Birchwood on Hwy. 48, then two miles south on Loch Lomand Boulevard
**Course:** 9 holes/par 36/3,232 yards
**Fee:** $$
**Amenities:** Driving range; restaurant; bar; motel

Third-oldest golf course in Wisconsin, expanding to 18 holes in the spring of 1996.

## TAHKODAH HILLS GC

#93 Lake Owen Dr. • Cable 54821 • 715/798-3760

**Directions:** Co. M east from Cable 2 3/4 miles to Lake Owen Drive, north on Lake Owen Drive 2 3/4 miles
**Course:** 9 holes/par 35/2,540 yards
**Fee:** $$

Nine more holes are being added to this course, next to the Chequamegon National Forest. The current nine, built in 1971, has undergone a lot of revision, with sand traps being added and holes being lengthened. The course features wide fairways, gentle slopes and majestic century-old pines.

*Madeline Island Golf Course in La Pointe*

## TAYLOR'S AMACOY GOLF & SUPPER CLUB

N2906 Hwy. 40 • Bruce 54819 • 715/868-6952

**Directions:** Twenty-five miles north of Bloomer on Hwy. 40
**Course:** 9 holes/par 33/2,600 yards
**Fee:** $

## TEE-A-WAY GOLF & SUPPER CLUB

1401 E. 11 St. North • Ladysmith 54848 • 715/532-3766

**Directions:** East of Ladysmith on Hwy. 8
**Course:** 9 holes/par 35/2,946 yards
**Fee:** $

This 72-year-old course features mature trees, wide fairways and undulating greens.

## TEE-HI CLUB

580 Tee-Hi Pl. • Medford 54451 • 715/748-3990

**Directions:** Off of Hwy. 13, west on Perkins Street, then left on Tee-Hi Place
**Course:** 9 holes/par 31/2,010 yards
**Fee:** $  Tee times required
**Amenities:** Newly expanded clubhouse

This course was built around 1930.

## TELEMARK GC

P.O. Box 277 • Cable 54821 • 715/798-3811

**Directions:** From the Twin Cities, I-35 north to Hwy. 8, east on Hwy. 8, then north on Hwy. 63 to Cable, west four miles
**Course:** 18 holes/par 72/6,403 yards
**Fee:** $$
**Amenities:** Full resort facility; practice fairway and green

Situated next to the Chequamegon National Forest, this 23-year-old course is set on gently rolling and densely wooded terrain. Thousands of pine, aspen, birch, maple, oak, cherry and poplar trees line this beautiful northwoods course. The layout features 22 sand traps, four water holes and—quite frequently—many white-tailed deer.

## TIMBER TERRACE GC

1117 Pumphouse Rd. • Chippewa Falls 54729 • 715/726-1500

**Directions:** Hwy. 124 to NSP Dam, Court Street, right on State Street to Pumphouse Road
**Course:** 9 holes/par 35/2,900 yards
**Fee:** $

**Amenities:** Golf cart and club rentals; restaurant

This fully irrigated course is located along the Chippewa River.

## TURTLEBACK GOLF & CC

West Allen Road • P.O. Box 363 • Rice Lake 54868 • 715/234-7641

**Directions:** One mile west of Rice Lake, off of Hwy. 53
**Course:** 18 holes/par 71/6,138 yards
**Fee:** $$    Tee times required
**Amenities:** Full-service clubhouse, including bar and grill and dining room; driving range; full-service pro shop with rental equipment; golf lessons available

The original nine-hole course, established in 1927, was called Hi-Dale for its high, rolling terrain cutting through towering hardwoods. In 1982, nine new holes were added, and the well-landscaped course was renamed Turtleback. The current layout has plenty of trees and water and enough length to challenge most recreational golfers. A feature hole is the 278-yard, par-4 ninth hole, which has water hazards. Try to beat Andy North's record: 64.

## VOYAGER VILLAGE CC

28851 Kilkare Rd. • Danbury 54830 • 715/259-3911

**Directions:** North of Hwy. 35 on Co. A, 16 miles east of Webster
**Course:** 18 holes/par 72/6,794 yards
**Fee:** $$
**Amenities:** Tennis courts; swimming pool; clubhouse

Narrow fairways wind through the trees with an airstrip running down the center of the course.

*Telemark Resort in Cable*

*Mill Run in Eau Claire*

## WESTWOOD GOLF & SUPPER CLUB

N8785 Golf Course Rd. • Phillips 54555 • 715/339-3600

**Directions:** West on Co. F, 1 1/2 miles from Hwy. 13 to Golf Course Road

**Course:** 9 holes/par 35/2,985 yards

**Fee:** $

**Amenities:** Log and fieldstone clubhouse with dining room dominated by a large stone fireplace; supper club open to public

Built around 1930, this course recently installed a new irrigation system and new tees. The course runs along the shores of Long Lake. Water comes into play on four holes. Sand traps, fairways lined with pine trees, and fast greens round out the challenge.

## WHISPERING PINES GC

Co. X • P.O. Box 332 • Cadott 54727 • 715/289-GOLF

**Directions:** One-half mile west of Cadott on Co. X

**Course:** 9 holes/par 36/3,320 yards

**Fee:** $

A second nine is being added to this course, which opened in the late 1980s. The current nine is fairly long with a 607-yard finishing hole. The course has large greens, some two-tiered, and gently rolling fairways, four very tight due to trees.

# WHITETAIL GC

Rural Route 3 • Colfax 54730 • 715/962-3888

**Directions:** Four miles north of I-94 on Hwy. 40, between Eau Claire and Menomonie
**Course:** 18 holes/par 71/6,427 yards
**Fee:** $

This course has undergone much revision with the addition of a second nine in 1992.

# YELLOW LAKE GC

7768 Co. U • Danbury 54830 • 715/866-7107

**Directions:** One mile west of Hwy. 35 between Danbury and Webster on Co. U
**Course:** 9 holes/par 34/2,627 yards
**Fee:** $
**Amenities:** Bar and grill; nine-hole mini-golf

This course, established in the 1920s, has sand greens—some of the last in the country. You can play just about anytime of year, provided you can swing in your snowmobile suit. Special "snow golf balls" and "glow-in-the-dark" balls (for night play) are available.

# Northeast Courses

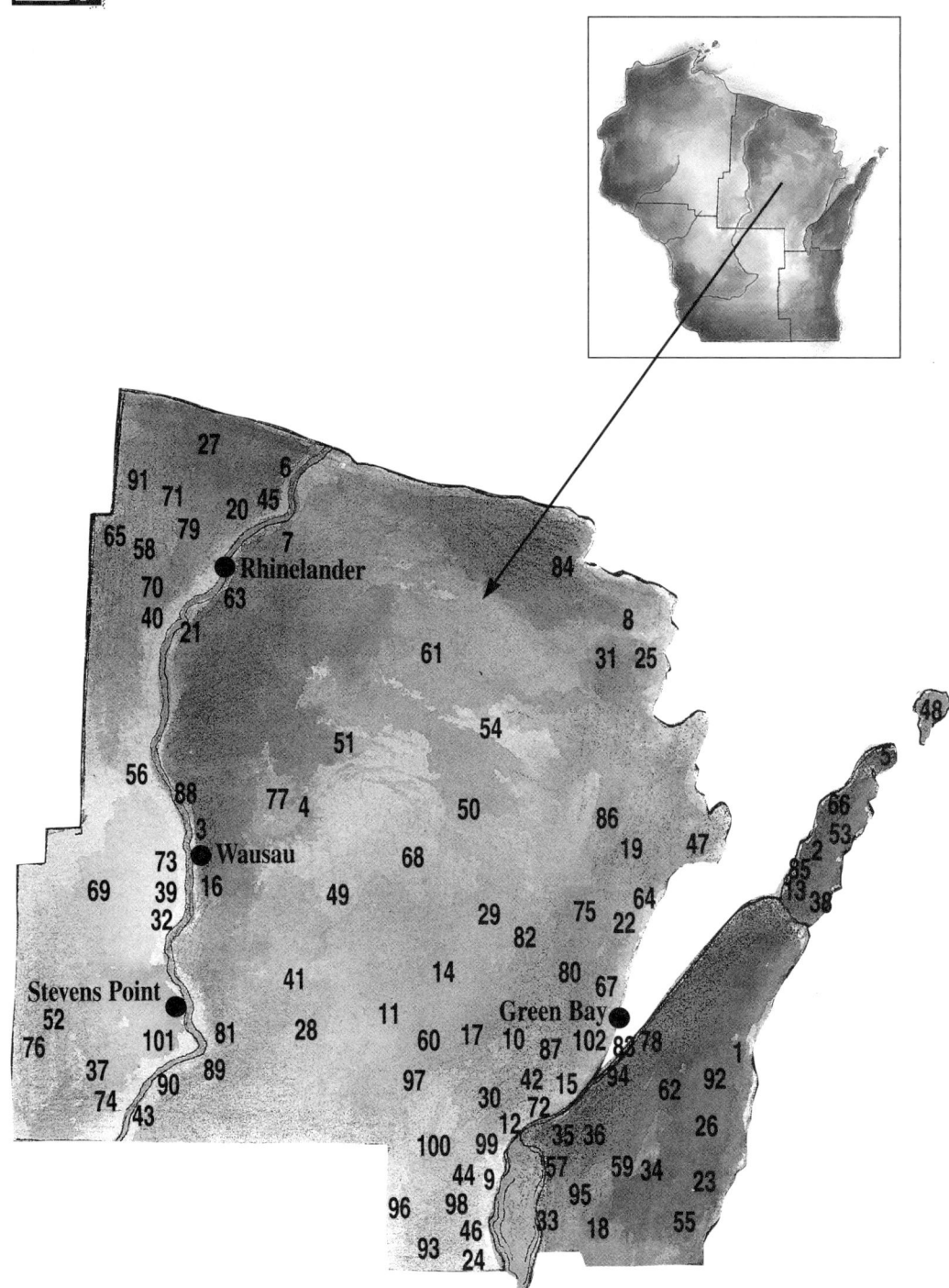

| No. | Page |
|---|---|
| 1 ALASKAN GOLF COURSE | 86 |
| 2 ALPINE GOLF COURSE | 86 |
| 3 AMERICAN LEGION GOLF COURSE | 86 |
| 4 ANTIGO BASS LAKE | 86 |
| 5 BAY RIDGE GOLF COURSE | 87 |
| 6 BIG SAND GOLF COURSE | 87 |
| 7 BIG STONE GOLF COURSE & COUNTRY CLUB | 87 |
| 8 BOMBERS BAR & GOLF | 87 |
| 9 BRIDGEWOOD GOLF COURSE | 87 |
| 10 BROWN COUNTY GOLF COURSE | 88 |
| 11 CEDAR SPRINGS GOLF COURSE | 88 |
| 12 CHASKA GOLF COURSE | 88 |
| 13 CHERRY HILLS GOLF COURSE | 88 |
| 14 CLINTONVILLE RIVERSIDE GOLF COURSE | 88 |
| 15 COUNTRY SIDE GOLF CLUB | 88 |
| 16 CRANE MEADOWS GOLF COURSE | 89 |
| 17 CRYSTAL SPRINGS GOLF COURSE | 89 |
| 18 DEER RUN COUNTRY CLUB | 89 |
| 19 DESMIDT'S GOLF COURSE & COUNTRY CLUB | 90 |
| 20 EAGLE RIVER MUNI GOLF COURSE | 90 |
| 21 EDGEWATER GOLF COURSE | 90 |
| 22 EDGEWOOD GOLF COURSE | 90 |
| 23 FAIRVIEW GOLF COURSE | 90 |
| 24 FAR VU GOLF COURSE | 91 |
| 25 FOUR SEASONS GOLF COURSE | 91 |
| 26 FOX HILLS RESORT | 91 |
| 27 GATEWAY GOLF COURSE | 91 |
| 28 GLEN CAIRN GOLF COURSE | 92 |
| 29 GOLDEN SANDS GOLF COURSE | 92 |
| 30 GRANDVIEW GOLF COURSE | 92 |
| 31 GREEN ACRES | 92 |
| 32 GREENWOOD HILLS COUNTRY CLUB | 92 |
| 33 HICKORY HILLS GOLF COURSE | 93 |
| 34 HIGH CLIFF GOLF COURSE | 93 |
| 35 HIGHLAND RIDGE GOLF COURSE | 93 |
| 36 HILLY HAVEN SKI & GOLF | 93 |
| 37 HOMESTEAD GOLF COURSE | 94 |
| 38 IDLEWILD GOLF COURSE OF DOOR COUNTY | 94 |
| 39 INDIANHEAD GOLF COURSE | 94 |
| 40 INSHALLA COUNTRY CLUB | 94 |
| 41 IOLA COMMUNITY GOLF COURSE | 95 |
| 42 IRISH WATERS GOLF COURSE | 95 |
| 43 LAKE ARROWHEAD GOLF COURSE | 95 |
| 44 LAKE BREEZE GOLF COURSE | 95 |
| 45 LAKE FOREST GOLF COURSE | 96 |
| 46 LAKE SHORE GOLF COURSE | 96 |
| 47 LITTLE RIVER COUNTRY CLUB | 96 |
| 48 MAPLE GROVE GOLF COURSE & RESORT | 96 |
| 49 MAPLE HILLS GOLF COURSE | 96 |
| 50 MAPLE VALLEY GOLF COURSE | 97 |
| 51 MAPLEWOOD GOLF COURSE | 97 |
| 52 MARSHFIELD COUNTRY CLUB | 98 |
| 53 MAXWELTON BRAES GOLF COURSE | 98 |
| 54 MCCAUSLIN BROOK GOLF COURSE | 98 |
| 55 MEADOW LINKS GOLF COURSE | 99 |
| 56 MERRILL GOLF COURSE | 99 |
| 57 MID-VALLEE GOLF COURSE | 99 |
| 58 MINOCQUA COUNTRY CLUB | 99 |
| 59 MYSTERY HILLS GOLF COURSE | 99 |
| 60 NEW LONDON GOLF COURSE | 100 |
| 61 NICOLET COUNTRY CLUB | 100 |
| 62 NORTHBROOK COUNTRY CLUB | 100 |
| 63 NORTHWOOD GOLF COURSE | 100 |
| 64 OCONTO GOLF COURSE | 100 |
| 65 PECK'S WILDWOOD GOLF COURSE | 101 |
| 66 PENINSULA STATE PARK GOLF COURSE | 101 |
| 67 PINE ACRES GOLF COURSE | 101 |
| 68 PINE HILLS COUNTRY CLUB | 101 |
| 69 PINE VALLEY GOLF COURSE | 102 |
| 70 PINEWOOD COUNTRY CLUB | 102 |
| 71 PLUM LAKE GOLF COURSE | 102 |
| 72 REID MUNICIPAL GOLF COURSE | 102 |
| 73 RIB MOUNTAIN GOLF COURSE | 103 |
| 74 RIDGES GOLF COURSE, THE | 103 |
| 75 RIVER ISLAND GOLF COURSE | 103 |
| 76 RIVEREDGE COUNTRY CLUB | 103 |
| 77 RIVERVIEW COUNTRY CLUB & GOLF COURSE | 104 |
| 78 ROYAL SCOT GOLF COURSE | 104 |
| 79 ST. GERMAIN GOLF COURSE | 104 |
| 80 SANDALWOOD COUNTRY CLUB | 104 |
| 81 SENTRYWORLD | 104 |
| 82 SHAWANO LAKE GOLF COURSE | 105 |
| 83 SHOREWOOD | 105 |
| 84 SPREAD EAGLE GOLF COURSE | 105 |
| 85 STONEHEDGE GOLF COURSE | 106 |
| 86 SUNDOWN GOLF COURSE | 106 |
| 87 THORNBERRY CREEK COUNTRY CLUB | 106 |
| 88 TRAPP RIVER GOLF COURSE | 106 |
| 89 TREE ACRES GOLF COURSE | 106 |
| 90 TRI-CITY GOLF COURSE | 107 |
| 91 TROUT LAKE GOLF & COUNTRY CLUB | 107 |
| 92 TWIN OAKS COUNTRY CLUB | 108 |
| 93 UTICA GOLF COURSE | 108 |
| 94 VILLAGE GREEN GOLF COURSE | 108 |
| 95 WANDER SPRINGS | 108 |
| 96 WEDGEWOOD SUPPER CLUB & GOLF COURSE | 109 |
| 97 WESTHAVEN GOLF COURSE | 109 |
| 98 WEYMONT RUN COUNTRY CLUB | 110 |
| 99 WINAGAMIE GOLF COURSE | 110 |
| 100 WINCHESTER HILLS GOLF COURSE | 110 |
| 101 WISCONSIN RIVER COUNTRY CLUB | 111 |
| 102 WOODSIDE COUNTRY CLUB | 111 |

*Great Golf in Wisconsin*

## ALASKAN GC

N6092 Hwy. 42 • Kewaunee 54216 • 414/388-3940

**Directions**: Thirty miles east of Green Bay between Kewaunee and Algoma
**Course:** 9 holes/par 36/2,839 yards
**Fee:** $    Tee times recommended
**Amenities:** Golf shop with bar; driving range

This older (1937) course in this Great Lakes port town is fairly flat with water coming into play on four of the holes. Smaller greens require a good short game.

## ALPINE GC

P.O. Box 200 • Egg Harbor 54209 • 414/868-3232

**Directions:** Three-quarters of a mile southeast of Egg Harbor on Co. G
**Course:** 27 holes/par 35/2,849 yards, par 36/3,198 yards, par 36/3,009 yards
**Fee:** $$
**Amenities:** Bar serving drinks and food; pro shop; golf packages

This scenic Door County course is best known for a tram that carries golfers to the top of a bluff, where a spectacular view of the bay can be seen. Many trees border the bluegrass fairways and bent greens.

## AMERICAN LEGION GC

Golf Club Road • Wausau 54401 • 715/675-3663

**Directions**: Northeast side of Wausau, North 6th Street to Golf Club Road
**Course:** 9 holes/par 34/2,821 yards
**Fee:** $    Tee times required

New fairways and a tee-to-green watering system are new at this course for 1994.

## ANTIGO BASS LAKE

RFD 2 • Deerbrook 54424 • 715/623-6201

**Directions:** Sixteen miles north of Antigo, off Hwy. 45 North
**Course:** 18 holes/par 71/6,161 yards
**Fee:** $$

**Amenities:** Restaurant; bar; pro shop

This is a fun, challenging resort course near the national forest and prime recreational lands.

## BAY RIDGE GC

1116 Little Sister Rd. • Sister Bay 54234 • 414/854-4085

**Directions:** Hwy. 42 between Ephraim and Sister Bay
**Course:** 9 holes/par 35/2,689 yards
**Fee:** $$
**Amenities:** Clubhouse serving sandwiches, snacks, beer and soda

In the heart of charming Door County, this well-manicured course is fully irrigated and has many trees.

## BIG SAND GC

Sand Lake Club Road • Phelps 54554 • 715/545-2484

**Directions:** Seven miles east of Phelps on Hwy. 17
**Course:** 9 holes/par 36/3,025 yards
**Fee:** $$

## BIG STONE G & CC

846 Golf Course Loop • Three Lakes 54562 • 715/546-2880

**Directions:** Four miles south of Three Lakes on Hwy. 32
**Course:** 9 holes/par 35/2,921 yards
**Fee:** $$
**Amenities:** Bar; pro shop

Located on a lake in Wisconsin's scenic northwoods, this course is an enjoyable one to play.

## BOMBERS BAR & GOLF

22200 Bombers • Niagra 54151 • 715/251-3110

**Directions:** Hwy. 41 north to Hwy. 8
**Course:** 9 holes/par 33/2,004 yards
**Fee:** $

## BRIDGEWOOD GC

Hwy. 41 at Cecil Street • Neenah 54956 • 414/722-9819

**Directions:** Right off of Hwy. 41
**Course:** 18 holes/par 71/6,030 yards
**Fee:** $

This course can be played rather quickly, and the greens are small to medium in size.

## BROWN COUNTY GC

897 Riverdale • Oneida 54155 • 414/497-1731

**Directions:** West of Green Bay on Co. J
**Course:** 18 holes/par 72/6,729 yards
**Fee:** $$

This scenic course is characterized by mature trees and manicured fairways.

## CEDAR SPRINGS GC

Route 1 • P.O. Box 64 • Manawa 54949 • 414/596-2905

**Directions:** Two miles east of Manawa on Co. O
**Course:** 9 holes/par 35/2,814 yards
**Fee:** $   Tee times required

## CHASKA GC

Hwys. 10 and 45 • Appleton 54912 • 414/757-5757

**Directions:** Hwy. 41 to Hwy. 10 west three miles, on corner of Hwys. 10 and 45
**Course:** 18 holes/par 72/6,854 yards
**Fee:** $$
**Amenities:** Practice facilities; snack bar; locker rooms; power carts

## CHERRY HILLS GC

5905 Dunn Rd. • Sturgeon Bay 54235 • 414/743-4222

**Directions:** Four miles north of Sturgeon Bay on Hwy. 42, left on Dunn Road (Co. P)
**Course:** 18 holes/par 72/6,163 yards
**Fee:** $$
**Amenities:** Driving range; pro shop; gourmet restaurant; 30-room lodge; power carts; lessons; limited tee times available

## CLINTONVILLE RIVERSIDE GC

P.O. Box 188 • Clintonville 54929 • 715/823-2991

**Directions:** From Clintonville, one-half mile north on Co. D, then one-half mile west on Golf Club Road
**Course:** 9 holes/par 36/3,125 yards
**Fee:** $$
**Amenities:** Bar; restaurant; practice green; driving range; locker rooms

This well-manicured course is open to the public at certain times. Call for availability.

## COUNTRY SIDE GC

W726 Weiler Rd. • Kaukauna 54130 • 414/766-2219

**Directions:** Located 2 miles east of Co. CE & Hwy. 55 intersection
**Course:** 18 holes/par 71/6,140 yards
**Fee:** $   Tee times required

## CRANE MEADOWS GC

Weston Ave. • Schofield 54476 • 715/355-1264

**Directions:** Co. J one mile west of Hwy. 29, nine miles east of Wausau
**Course:** 9 holes/par 35/3,000 yards
**Fee:** $

## CRYSTAL SPRINGS GC

Route 2, French Road • Seymour 54165 • 414/833-6348 or 800/686-2984

**Directions:** Fifteen minutes west of Green Bay on Hwy. 54
**Course:** 18 holes/par 72/6,576 yards
**Fee:** $$
**Amenities:** Driving range; pro shop; restaurant; clubhouse

## DEER RUN CC

912 Fairway Dr. • Brillion 54110 • 414/756-2528

**Directions:** Two miles south of Hwy. 10 on Co. PP in Brillion
**Course:** 9 holes/par 36/3,200 yards
**Fee:** $

This nine-hole course is situated on natural, rolling terrain. Water comes into play on five holes. There is an abundance of young and mature trees. Well-placed sand bunkers will catch errant shots. The course is fully irrigated with bluegrass fairways and bentgrass greens and tees.

*Lake Arrowhead Golf Course in Nekoosa*

## DESMIDT'S GC & CC

Route 3, Shaffer Road • Crivitz 54114 • 715/854-7939

**Directions:** Co. A, four miles east from the junction of Hwy. 141 and Co. A
**Course:** 9 holes/par 29/1,750 yards
**Fee:** $$

Built in 1964, this manicured course is set in rolling terrain punctuated with flower beds and white sand bunkers.

## EAGLE RIVER MUNI GC

527 McKinley Blvd.• Eagle River 54521 • 715/479-8111 or 800/280-1477

**Directions:** Hwy. 45, one-quarter mile north of Eagle River on McKinley Boulevard
**Course:** 18 holes/par 71/6,069 yards
**Fee:** $$   Tee times required
**Amenities:** Pro shop; restaurant; full-service bar; driving range; practice green

This course is well-groomed and bunkered, offering challenging, narrow and forested fairways with water hazards. Take your best swing and watch for wildlife crossing the fairways.

## EDGEWATER GC

N10369 Echo Valley Rd. • Tomahawk 54487 • 715/453-3320

**Directions:** One mile east of Hwy. 51 on Co. A
**Course:** 9 holes/par 36/3,235 yards
**Fee:** $
**Amenities:** Equipment and golf cart rentals; cocktails; food; driving range; practice green

Built in 1928, this recently remodeled course features water on three holes.

## EDGEWOOD GC

2946 Logtown Rd. • Oconto 54153 • 414/834-2681

**Directions:** Two miles northwest of intersection of Hwys. 41 and 22
**Course:** 9 holes/par 36/3,030 yards
**Fee:** $

## FAIRVIEW GC

3659 Riverview Dr. • Two Rivers 54241 • 414/794-8726

**Directions:** Hwy. 42, north of city limits

**Course:** 9 holes/par 36/3,160 yards
**Fee:** $
**Amenities**: Driving range; subdivision; condos; sandwiches and drinks

This course added a new irrigation system in 1990 and may add nine more holes in the future.

## FAR VU GC

4985 State Rd. 175 • Oshkosh 54901 • 414/231-2631

**Directions:** Hwy. 175 between Oshkosh and Fond du Lac
**Course:** 18 holes/par 71/6,191 yards
**Fee:** $
**Amenities:** Bar; pro shop

This course sports enlarged greens and watered fairways and will give you the opportunity to use most, if not all, of your irons.

## FOUR SEASONS GC

Pembine 54156 • 715/324-5244

**Directions**: Seven miles east of Hwy. 141
**Course:** 9 holes/par 34/2,670 yards
**Fee:** $

This course will have added bunkers and sand traps for the 1994 season.

## FOX HILLS RESORT

300 Church St. • Mishicot 54228 • 800/955-7615

**Directions:** North of Manitowoc, off I-43, exits 164 or 154
**Course:** 45 holes/par 72/6,147 yards, par 72/6,267 yards, par 35/2,920 yards
**Fee:** $$    Tee times required
**Amenities:** Hotel; condos; restaurants; locker room; two pro shops; convention and meeting facilities; two indoor and two outdoor swimming pools

## GATEWAY GC

4146 Co. B • Land O'Lakes 54540 • 715/547-3929

**Directions:** West of Hwy. 45
**Course:** 9 holes/par 36/3,378 yards
**Fee:** $$
**Amenities:** Pro shop; full bar; practice range

Deep bunkers and large greens best describe this northwoods course.

 ***Bring your own barrel.*** *A manmade waterfall plunges 30 feet at NorthWood GC in Rhinelander.*

***Just don't chase the ball.*** *At Alpine Golf Course in Egg Harbor a tram carries you to the top of the bluff for a spectacular view of bay waters below.*

## GLEN CAIRN GC

N9254 Campbell Lake Rd. • Ogdensburg 54962 • 414/244-GOLF

**Directions:** Twenty miles north of Waupaca on Hwy. E to Co. OO
**Course:** 9 holes/par 36/2,800 yards
**Fee:** $

## GOLDEN SANDS GC

300 Nabor Rd. • Cecil 54111 • 715/745-2189

**Directions:** Hwy. 22 and Co. R, 35 miles from Green Bay
**Course:** 18 holes/par 70/6,300 yards
**Fee:** $$    Tee times required
**Amenities:** New banquet facility and dining room; fully equipped pro shop; two golf pros

## GRANDVIEW GC

333 N. Oak St. • Hortonville 54944 • 414/779-6421

**Directions:** One-half mile north of Hwy. 45 on Co. M
**Course:** 9 holes/par 35/2,816 yards
**Fee:** $    Tee times required on weekends
**Amenities:** Clubhouse addition in 1993; party and banquet facility new for 1994

## GREEN ACRES

Route 1 • Pembine 54156 • 715/324-5707

**Directions:** East of Hwy. 141
**Course:** 9 holes/par 34/5,020 yards
**Fee:** $
**Amenities:**  Cocktail lounge; practice green

This somewhat hilly course is nestled in the northwoods and offers variety to golfers.

## GREENWOOD HILLS CC

2002 Poplar Lane • Wausau 54403 • 715/848-2204

**Directions:** Exit Hwy. 29 east at Co. X (Camp Phillips Road), 5 miles north to Co. N (Town Line Road). Turn left (west) 1/2 mile to Poplar Lane

**Course:** 9 holes/par 36/3,475 yards
**Fee:** $$

This is a new course (opened fall 1993), with a second nine to open in late summer 1994. Carved from a magnificent piece of land, it boasts a challenging mixture of rolling terrain and fairways lined with mature trees.

## HICKORY HILLS GC

W3095 Hickory Hills Rd. • Chilton 53014 • 414/849-2912 or 800/236-2911

**Directions:** Two miles north of Chilton on Hwy. 57
**Course:** 18 holes/par 71/6,066 yards
**Fee:** $
**Amenities:** Pro shop; driving range; food & beverages.

This sporty course is fun to play.

## HIGH CLIFF GC

W5055 Golf Course Rd. • Sherwood 54169 • 414/989-1045

**Directions:** One mile off Hwys. 114 and 55
**Course:** 18 holes/par 71/6,142 yards
**Fee:** $    Tee times required
**Amenities:** Twenty condo-tels; restaurant; bar and grill

## HIGHLAND RIDGE GC

1106 Sand Acres Dr. • De Pere 54115 • 414/337-9986

**Directions:** Three-quarters of a mile west of Hwy. 41 on Co. G (Main Street, De Pere), then south one block on Sand Acres Drive
**Course:** 9 holes/par 36/3,385 yards
**Fee:** $
**Amenities:** Clubhouse; bar; sandwiches; pro shop; driving range

This is a fairly open course with an interesting layout, and it will be adding a second nine holes in the fall of 1994.

## HILLY HAVEN SKI & GOLF

5911 Co. PP • De Pere 54115 • 414/336-6204

**Directions:** 6 1/2 miles south of De Pere on County Hwy. PP
**Course:** 9 holes/par 35/2,936 yards
**Fee:** $    Tee times required

Built 25 years ago on pleasantly rolling, wooded terrain, this picturesque course takes in a trickling creek, natural waterfall and limestone formations. The course is tougher than its length would indicate due to water (comes into play on seven holes) and new sand traps. A second nine is planned.

## HOMESTEAD GC

3372 Hwy. 13 North • Wisconsin Rapids 54495 • 715/423-7577

**Directions:** Hwy. 13 north from Wisconsin Rapids
**Course:** 9 holes/par 34/2,712 yards
**Fee:** $
**Amenities:** Pro shop; full service restaurant; driving range

Built in 1971 on an old farm, this short course is easy to walk. It has few trees but lots of water.

## IDLEWILD GC OF DOOR COUNTY

4146 Golf Valley Dr. • Sturgeon Bay 54235 • 414/743-3334

**Directions:** Hwy. 42/57 to Idlewild Road to Hainesville Road to Golf Valley Drive
**Course:** 18 holes/par 72/6,954 yards
**Fee:** $$
**Amenities:** Pro shop, range, lounge, glass solarium overlooking course

This course is nestled in a scenic valley setting.

## INDIANHEAD GC

966 Indianhead Dr. • Mosinee 54455 • 715/693-6066

**Directions:** Off Hwy. 51, across from Central Wisconsin Airport
**Course:** 18 holes/par 72/6,530 yards
**Fee:** $$    Tee times required

A new, distinct nine is to open at this course in the spring of '94. The new nine and redesigned old nine were the work of Bob Lohman's design group. The front nine is long but open; the back nine is shorter with tree-lined fairways throughout. The 134-yard sixth hole is a look-alike of Augusta's No. 12. Another interesting hole is No. 16, a crescent-shaped par-5 where either sand or water can come into play all the way to the small green.

## INSHALLA CC

N11060 Clear Lake Rd. • Tomahawk 54487 • 715/453-3130

**Directions:** Two miles north of Tomahawk on Business Hwy. 51 to Co. U, then one-half mile to Clear Lake Road
**Course:** 18 holes/par 70/5,599 yards
**Fee:** $$

This course offers short yet fun, challenging golf in a parklike setting that boasts many tall trees, small ponds and rolling terrain. Don't let the distance fool you. After five years of 18-hole play, the course record is only a two-under-par 68. The course has large, undulating bentgrass greens.

## IOLA COMMUNITY GC

Route 2 • Iola 54945 • 715/445-3831

**Directions:** North of Hwy. 161 on Co. J, 13 miles north of Waupaca

**Course:** 9 holes/par 36/3,205 yards

**Fee:** $$

**Amenities:** Full-service clubhouse; driving range; practice green; club rental

Built in the late 1960s, this course covers hills and flatlands filled with pines and hardwoods. A large pond and 20 sand traps make things interesting for those who take advantage of the large greens and wide fairways.

## IRISH WATERS GC

W2896 Co. S • Kaukauna 54130 • 414/734-8017

**Directions:** 1 3/4 miles west of Hwy. 55 on Co. S

**Course:** 18 holes/par 72/7,100 yards

**Fee:** $$

**Amenities:** Pro shop; snack bar; pro on staff

Water can be found on 11 of this course's 18 holes, and there is an island green to test your accuracy.

## LAKE ARROWHEAD GC

1195 Apache Ln. • Nekoosa 54457 • 715/325-2929

**Directions:** On Hwy. 13, 35 miles north of Wisconsin Dells, 13 miles south of Wisconsin Rapids

**Course:** 18 holes/par 72/6,624 yards

**Fee:** $$$

**Amenities:** Full practice facilities; restaurant/lounge; tennis; pools; sauna; camping

## LAKE BREEZE GC

6333 Hwy. 110 • Winneconne 54986 • 414/582-7585

**Directions:** Eight miles north of Hwys. 41 and 110, exit on Hwy. 110

**Course:** 18 holes/par 72/6,896 yards

**Fee:** $

**Amenities:** Driving range; putting and chipping areas; lounge; bar; restaurant; pro shop

Designed by Homer Fieldhouse, this course was built in 1990. It blends in well with the natural beauty of the area, challenging golfers with 32 sand traps and five lakes. You'll remember the No. 1 hole, with a green shaped like the state of Wisconsin.

*Great Golf in Wisconsin*

## LAKE FOREST GC

3801 Eagle Waters Rd. • Eagle River 54521 • 715/479-4211

**Directions:** Hwy. 70, 4 1/2 miles east of Eagle River, left on Range Line Road
**Course:** 9 holes/par 36/2,875 yards
**Fee:** $$

## LAKE SHORE GC

2175 Punhoqua Rd. • Oshkosh 54901 • 414/235-6200

**Directions:** Hwy. 41 to Hwy. 21, east one mile to Punhoqua Road, then north one mile
**Course:** 18 holes/par 70/6,030 yards
**Fee:** $   Tee times required on weekends and holidays

This is a course with some very challenging holes for golfers of all abilities.

## LITTLE RIVER CC

N2235 Shore Dr. • Marinette 54143 • 715/735-7234

**Directions:** Hwys. 41 and 64 juncture with Cleveland or Co. T to Shore Drive, then south two miles
**Course:** 18 holes/par 71/6,060 yards
**Fee:** $$   Tee times required
**Amenities:** Driving range

This old course (built in 1927), located by a Lake Michigan bay, is a scenic track that features lots of water, tree-lined fairways, fast bentgrass greens and abundant wildlife. More bunkers are being added to the 20 sand traps that are there now.

## MAPLE GROVE GC & RESORT

Main and Michigan Roads • Washington Island 54246 • 414/847-2017

**Directions:** Hwy. 42 to Northport at end of Door Peninsula, ferry to island, then Ferry Dock Road to Main Road, north 1 1/2 miles
**Course:** 9 holes/par 35/2,814 yards
**Fee:** $$   (18-hole rate)
**Amenities:** 18-hole mini-golf; three-unit motel; restaurant; putting green

Small greens and woods make golfing on this Lake Michigan island a real Wisconsin experience. This course was built in 1969.

## MAPLE HILLS GC

Route 2 • Wittenberg 54499 • 715/253-2448

**Directions:** East of Wittenberg, intersection of Hwys. 45 and 29

**Course:** 9 holes/par 36/2,850 yards
**Fee:** $$
**Amenities:** Pro shop; practice green; restaurant & bar

This wooded course will challenge you with large greens and deep bunkers, and its rolling hills make for a scenic round.

## MAPLE VALLEY GC

529 Golf Course Rd. • Suring 54174 • 414/842-2525

**Directions:** Hwy. 32, about 50 miles northwest of Green Bay
**Course:** 9 holes/par 35/2,642 yards
**Fee:** $
**Amenities:** Driving range

This course, built in 1962, is in a natural setting featuring rolling terrain, small greens and lots of trees. Five water hazards and five bunkers make it interesting.

## MAPLEWOOD GC

Hwy. 55 and Twin View Drive • Pickerel 54465 • 715/484-GOLF

**Directions:** Hwy. 55 to Pickerel
**Course:** 9 holes/par 36/3,073 yards
**Fee:** $
**Amenities:** New clubhouse; bar and restaurant; pro shop

On Big Twin Lake in Langlade County, this newer course (built in 1985) is located in one of the state's prettiest regions.

*NorthWood Golf Course in Rhinelander*

## MARSHFIELD CC

11426 Hwy. B • Marshfield 54449 • 715/384-4409

**Directions:** Two miles west of Marshfield on Co. H
**Course:** 18 holes/par 70/6,004 yards
**Fee:** $
**Amenities:** Driving range; PGA lessons aided by video; computer clubmaking; pro shop; clubhouse

This course has two nines—the first built in 1922, the second in 1974. It also has many natural bentgrass fairways, water, trees and 13 bunkers.

## MAXWELTON BRAES GC

Hwy. 57 • Baileys Harbor 54202 • 414/839-2321

**Directions:** 1 mile south of Baileys Harbor on Hwy. 57
**Course:** 18 holes/par 71/6,045 yards
**Fee:** $$
**Amenities:** Pro shop

## McCAUSLIN BROOK GC

17067 Clubhouse Ln. • Lakewood 54138 • 715/276-7623

**Directions:** One mile out of Lakewood on Co. F
**Course:** 18 holes/par 70/5,926
**Fee:** $
**Amenities:** Pro shop; supper club; airport

This course, although not too lengthy, provides lots of challenge. The country's oldest logging camp on its original site can be found here.

*The Ridges Golf Course in Wisconsin Rapids*

## MEADOW LINKS GC

1540 Johnston Dr. • Manitowoc 54220 • 414/682-6842

**Directions:** Hwy. 42 to Johnston Drive, one-half mile north
**Course:** 18 holes/par 72/5,934 yards
**Fee:** $
**Amenities:** Bowling center; pro shop; restaurant

This is a short, fairly open course.

## MERRILL GC

1604 O'Day St. • Merrill 54452 • 715/536-2529

**Directions:** Hwy. 51 north to Hwy. 64, west two miles to Hwy. K to O'Day Street. Course is 2 blocks on right.
**Course:** 18 holes/par 71/6,450 yards
**Fee:** $$

## MID-VALLEE GC

3134 Apple Creek Rd. • De Pere 54115 • 414/532-6644 or 414/532-6674

**Directions:** Hwy. 41 halfway between Appleton and Green Bay
**Course:** 18 holes/par 72/6,653 yards
**Fee:** $$
**Amenities:** Complete golf shop; bar & short-order kitchen; pitching & putting greens

A beautiful, maturing golf course with plenty of trees, water and other hazards to challenge even the best golfer.

## MINOCQUA CC

9299 Country Club Rd. • Minocqua 54548 • 715/356-5217 or 715/356-5216

**Directions:** Hwy. 51 to Country Club Road on the south end of the Lake Minocqua bridge, then two miles east on Country Club Road
**Course:** 9 holes/par 35/2,784 yards
**Fee:** $$$    Tee times and carts required

This older course (built in 1923) has new tees for 1994.

## MYSTERY HILLS GC

3149 Dickinson Rd. • De Pere 54115 • 414/336-6077

**Directions:** Co. GV exit 172, south to Co. G, then left 1 1/2 miles
**Courses:** 18 holes/par 72/6,323 yards, 9 holes/par 32/1,851 yards
**Fee:** $$

## NEW LONDON GC

Route 5, Hwy. 45 North • New London 54961 • 414/982-9993

**Directions:** Two miles north of New London on Hwy. 45
**Course:** 9 holes/par 35/3,088 yards
**Fee:** $   Tee times required

This older course (built in 1926) has lots of mature oaks and pines, watered fairways, greens and tee boxes.

## NICOLET CC

Route 1 • P. O. Box 56 • Laona 54541 • 715/674-4780

**Directions:** One-half mile west of Laona on Hwy. 8
**Course:** 18 holes/par 67/4,553 yards
**Fee:** $
**Amenities:** New driving range; clubhouse; restaurant; PGA assistant

This executive course was first established in 1960. A back nine, a par 32, was added in 1980. This nine features narrow bentgrass fairways.

## NORTHBROOK CC

407 NorthBrook Dr. • Luxemburg 54217 • 414/845-2306

**Directions:** North on Hwys. 54/57, east on Hwy. 54, nine miles to Luxemburg, then left one mile on Co. A
**Course:** 18 holes/par 71/6,090 yards
**Fee:** $$
**Amenities:** Pro shop

## NORTHWOOD GC

6301 Hwy. 8 West • Rhinelander 54501 • 715/282-6565

**Directions:** Three miles west of Rhinelander on Hwy. 8
**Course:** 18 holes/par 72/6,719 yards
**Fee:** $$
**Amenities:** Pro shop; snack bar; driving range

This scenic course winds its way through the beautiful northwoods and features two island greens.

## OCONTO GC

532 Jefferson • Oconto 54153 • 414/834-3139

**Directions:** One mile east of Hwy. 41
**Course:** 9 holes/par 36/3,030 yards
**Fee:** $
**Amenities:** Bar; supper club

This is a wooded, fairly flat northwoods course.

## PECK'S WILDWOOD GC

10080 Hwy. 70 West • Minocqua 54548 • 715/356-3477

**Directions:** Two miles west of Hwy. 51 on Hwy. 70 in Minocqua
**Course:** 18 holes/par 72/6,120 yards
**Fee:** $$
**Amenities:** Practice range and green; locker rooms; club rental; pro shop; clubhouse with bar and food service

This relatively new course (built in two stages in the 1980s) meanders over gently rolling terrain near the Tomahawk River. Water can come into play on nine holes, most notably on the 530-yard, par-5 14th hole. There's also a 630-yard par 5, the fifth hole, that has a pond with which to contend. You must be tough for this course. The course record as of 1993: 77.

## PENINSULA STATE PARK GC

Hwy. 42 • P.O. Box 218 • Fish Creek 54212 • 414/854-5791

**Directions:** Three miles north of Fish Creek on Hwy. 42
**Course:** 18 holes/par 71/6,224 yards
**Fee:** $$

## PINE ACRES GC

3235 Sot Rd. • Abrams 54101 • 414/826-7765

**Directions:** Twenty miles north of Green Bay where Hwys. 41 and 141 split at Abrams
**Course:** 9 holes/par 33/2,400 yards
**Fee:** $
**Amenities:** Clubhouse

## PINE HILLS CC

N4698 Big Lake Rd. • Gresham 54128 • 715/787-3778

**Directions:** Eighteen miles northwest of Shawano
**Course:** 9 holes/par 36/3,056 yards
**Fee:** $$
**Amenities:** Driving range; putting green; restaurant; bar

This is a relatively flat course, nicely landscaped. A new course is being redesigned with a new 18 for 1995.

***And a few bees.*** *Over 90,000 flowers can be found on the famed flower hole (No. 16) at SentryWorld in Stevens Point. In all, the course contains more than five acres of flowers.*

*No lutefisk–we promise.* Peninsula State Park Golf Course in Door County is carved out of an old Norwegian farmstead.

## PINE VALLEY GC

203 136th Ave. North • Marathon 54448 • 715/443-2848

**Directions:** Eight miles west of Wausau on Hwy. 29
**Course:** 9 holes/par 35/2,837 yards
**Fee:** $

This well-maintained course is located amid the woods, streams, rolling hills and farms of central Wisconsin. Built in 1967, with two new holes for 1994, the course has bluegrass fairways and bentgrass greens.

## PINEWOOD CC

4660 Lakewood Rd. • Harshaw 54529 • 715/282-5500 or 800/746-3963

**Directions:** Hwy. 51, 13 miles south of Minocqua, left on Rocky Run Road, then left on Lakewood Road to clubhouse
**Course:** 18 holes/par 72/6,206 yards
**Fee:** $$    Tee times required in June, July and August
**Amenities:** Airport; cottages; restaurant serving lunch and dinner; golf learning center; dinner theatre; pro shop; showers

Bearskin trout stream, wooded hills and abundant wildlife are just a few of the unique features this course offers.

## PLUM LAKE GC

3160 Club House Rd. • Sayner 54560 • 715/542-9315

**Directions:** One mile east of Sayner off Co. N
**Course:** 9 holes/par 36/3,095 yards
**Fee:** $$$
**Amenities:** Driving range; snack shop; full pro shop

This course, one of the state's oldest, was built around 1910 by Fred James, father of 1902 U.S. Amateur Champion Louis S. James. Deer, bear and fox are frequently spotted crossing the course, a favorite of longtime visitors to northern Wisconsin.

## REID MUNICIPAL GC

1100 E. Fremont St. • Appleton 54915 • 414/832-5926

**Directions:** Hwy. 41 to College Avenue exit east, turn right on

Lawe Street, left on Fremont
**Course:** 18 holes/par 71/5,942 yards
**Fee:** $

The terrain on the front nine of this course is fairly flat, but the back nine has some rolling hills.

## RIB MOUNTAIN GC

3607 N. Mountain Rd., Co. NN • Wausau 54401 • 715/845-5570

**Directions:** One mile west of Hwys. 51 and 29 on Co. NN
**Course:** 9 holes/par 32/1,900 yards
**Fee:** $
**Amenities:** Driving range; restaurant

Located at the foot of Rib Mountain, this course is scenic and offers a great view.

## THE RIDGES GC

2311 Griffith Ave. • Wisconsin Rapids 54494 • 715/424-1111

**Directions:** South edge of Wisconsin Rapids
**Course:** 18 holes/par 72/6,338 yards
**Fee:** $$   Carts required on weekends in the summer
**Amenities:** Full practice facilities; lounge and grill; banquet and meeting rooms; pro shop

## RIVER ISLAND GC

P.O. Box 143 • Oconto Falls 54154 • 414/846-3303

**Directions:** Hwy. 22 to South Main to Mead Avenue to River Island Drive
**Course:** 9 holes/par 35/3,024 yards
**Fee:** $
**Amenities:** Pro shop; bar

The Oconto River runs through this course, so there are a number of water hazards.

## RIVEREDGE CC

10191 Mill Creek Rd. • Marshfield 54449 • 715/676-3900

**Directions:** Hwy. 13 north to Hwy. 10 west to Neillsville, 1 1/4 miles to Co. B north, then three-quarters of a mile to Mill Creek Road
**Course:** 18 holes/par 72/6,514 yards
**Fee:** $$
**Amenities:** Pro shop

## RIVERVIEW CC & GC

W11817 Highland Rd. • Antigo 54409 • 715/623-2663

**Directions:** Four miles west of Antigo on Hwy. 64
**Course:** 9 holes/par 36/3,120 yards
**Fee:** $
**Amenities:** Driving range; pro shop; full dining; lounge

This relatively flat course, built in 1963, features tree-lined fairways and several holes that cross water.

## ROYAL SCOT GC

4831 Church Rd. • New Franken 54229 • 414/866-2356

**Directions:** Three miles north of Green Bay, just off Hwy. 57
**Course:** 18 holes/par 72/6,572 yards
**Fee:** $$
**Amenities:** Restaurant with catering services

## ST. GERMAIN GC

9041 Hwy. 70 West • St. Germain 54558 • 715/542-2614

**Directions:** From Minocqua, Hwy. 51 north to Hwy. 70 east for eight miles, or from Eagle River, Hwy. 70 west through St. Germain for three miles
**Course:** 9 holes/par 36/3,119 yards
**Fee:** $$     Tee times required
**Amenities:** Whitetail Inn restaurant, made from 200-year-old pines, overlooks the ninth hole; full pro shop; driving range; group instruction

This new course, cut out of towering pines, is very tight. Keep the driver in the bag.

## SANDALWOOD CC

2954 Sandalwood Rd. • Abrams 54101 • 414/826-7770

**Directions:** Nineteen miles north of Green Bay, Hwy. 41/141 to Abrams, west three miles, between Co. D and Co. E on Sandalwood Road
**Course:** 18 holes/par 72/6,064 yards
**Fee:** $
**Amenities:** Restaurant; lounge

Built in 1974, this course has been updated with new ponds, new bunkers and new landscaping.

## SENTRYWORLD

601 Michigan Ave. • Stevens Point 54481 • 715/345-1600

**Directions:** Adjacent to Sentry Insurance Headquarters, north of city
**Course:** 18 holes/par 72/7,055 yards
**Fee:** $$$$    Tee times required
**Amenities:** Pro shop; golf lessons; restaurant; club making and repair; tennis; racquetball; squash; fishing; swimming; meeting rooms; banquets; lodging

## SHAWANO LAKE GC

W5714 Lake Dr. • Shawano 54166 • 715/524-4890

**Directions:** On Co. H, north shore of Shawano Lake across from the Shawano County Park
**Course:** 18 holes/par 71/6,201 yards
**Fee:** $$
**Amenities:** New grooming equipment; remodeled clubhouse; lounge; private meeting facilities; practice range

Old-course charm and many mature oak trees can be found at this one, built in 1922. The course, with small bentgrass greens, offers a wide variety of holes that feature hills, water and bunkers.

## SHOREWOOD

UW-Green Bay • 2420 Nicolet Drive • Green Bay 54311 • 414/465-2118

**Directions:** Hwys. 54-57 north or University Avenue north to Nicolet, third campus entrance
**Course:** 9 holes/par 35/3,006 yards
**Fee:** $
**Amenities:** Clubhouse

This wooded course is characterized by challenging, narrow, watered fairways and is quite hilly.

## SPREAD EAGLE GC

HC 2 • P. O. Box 234 • Spread Eagle 54121 • 715/696-3696

**Directions:** 8 miles west of Iron Mountain, Mich., at Hwy. 2 and 141
**Course:** 9 holes/par 36/2,657 yards
**Fee:** $
**Amenities:** New driving range

This course, carved out of towering oaks and pines, was built in the early 1970s, and has been updated with irrigation, new greens and new tees. The well-groomed course has enough water, sand and other hazards to challenge most golfers.

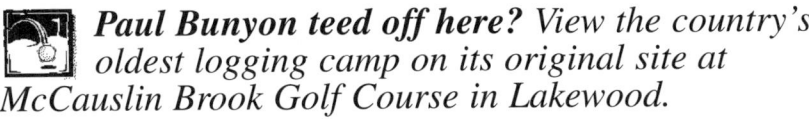

*Paul Bunyon teed off here?* View the country's oldest logging camp on its original site at McCauslin Brook Golf Course in Lakewood.

## STONEHEDGE GC

Co. E • Egg Harbor 54209 • 414/868-2566 or 868-3929

**Directions:** One mile east of Egg Harbor on Co. E
**Course:** 9 holes/par 34/2,175 yards
**Fee:** $
**Amenities:** Driving range; food and drinks at clubhouse

Short par 4s characterize this new course (opened in 1993), located on beautiful rolling terrain in the heart of Wisconsin's Door County. A big pond comes into play on three holes.

## SUNDOWN GC

Rural Route 4 • P.O. Box 215 • Crivitz 54114 • 715/854-7833

**Directions:** Two miles north of Crivitz on Hwy. 141, two miles west at sign
**Course:** 27 holes/par 33/2,125 yards, par 36/2,725 yards, par 36/2,763 yards
**Fee:** $
**Amenities:** Bar; pro shop

This 27-hole course is irrigated and tests golfers with lots of trees and hilly terrain.

## THORNBERRY CREEK CC

4470 N. Pine Tree Rd. • Oneida 54155 • 414/434-7501

**Directions:** Hwy. 29 west of Green Bay, 3 miles south on Sunlite, left on Pine Tree
**Course:** 9 holes/par 36/3,081 yards
**Fee:** $$
**Amenities:** Driving range

Unique nine-hole double green makes for a memorable round of 18.

## TRAPP RIVER GC

Hwy. WW • Wausau 54401 • 715/675-3044

**Directions:** Ten miles northeast of Wausau on CO. WW
**Course:** 18 holes/par 70/5,939 yards
**Fee:** $$

## TREE ACRES GC

5754 Pleasant Dr. • Plover 54467 • 715/341-4530

**Directions:** Hwy. 51 to Co. B in Plover, one-half mile east to Eisenhower, then one mile to Pleasant Drive
**Course:** 9 holes/par 36/2,800 yards
**Fee:** $$

**Amenities:** Full-service pro shop; lounge; patio; restaurant; driving range

Pretty, wooded, short course that is good for beginners and seniors.

## TRI-CITY GC

3000 Golf Course Rd. • Wisconsin Rapids 54494 • 715/423-1380

**Directions:** One mile west of Hwy. 13 between Grand Rapids and Wisconsin Rapids
**Course:** 9 holes/par 34/2,814 yards
**Fee:** $$
**Amenities:** Driving range; bar; snacks

This is a fairly flat course with quite a few trees.

## TROUT LAKE G & CC

AV3800 Hwy. 51 North • Woodruff 54568 • 715/385-2189

**Directions:** Ten miles north of Woodruff on Hwy. 51
**Course:** 18 holes/par 72/6,175 yards
**Fee:** $$
**Amenities:** Drinks and snacks at clubhouse with lovely veranda

Built in the mid-1920s, this course is especially pretty on the wooded back nine. The Trout River comes into play on several holes.

*SentryWorld at Stevens Point*

## TWIN OAKS CC

4871 Co. R • Denmark 54208 • 414/863-2716

**Directions:** Off I-43 at Denmark exit, six miles south
of Green Bay
**Course:** 18 holes/par 72/6,281 yards
**Fee:** $
**Amenities:** Golf bar and grill; driving range; locker rooms; pro shop

This course has two distinct nines. Accuracy is rewarded on the shorter front nine. The par-3 third hole, for example, requires a 135-yard shot from a cliff over a creek. Distance is rewarded on the longer back nine.

## UTICA GC

2330 Knott Rd. • Oshkosh 54903 • 414/233-4446

**Directions:** Hwy. 44 west of Hwy. 41 to Co. X, west to
Knott Road approximately three miles, then south
one-quarter mile
**Course:** 18 holes/par 71/6,018 yards
**Fee:** $   Tee times required on weekends and holidays
**Amenities:** Driving range; pro shop; bar

Built in 1975, this course planted many trees and fixed many new tees over the years and continues to do so today.

## VILLAGE GREEN GC

302 Riverdale • Green Bay 54313 • 414/434-3939

**Directions:** One mile west of Green Bay on Hwy. 29,
right on Riverdale
**Course:** 9 holes/par 36/3,259 yards
**Fee:** $

This course was built in 1968.

## WANDER SPRINGS

4342 Wayside Rd. • Greenleaf 54126 • 414/864-4653

**Directions:** Two miles east of Wayside on Wayside Road,
a short drive from Appleton, Green Bay, Two Rivers and
Manitowoc
**Course:** 18 holes/par 72/6,580 yards
**Fee:** $   Tee times required
**Amenities:** Practice range; bar; food; complete pro shop

This new course (the second nine opened in 1990) has three distinct sets of tees for golfers of all skills. The course is relatively level but has plenty of trees and water, which can come into play on at least seven holes. Other features include a large garden around the 17th hole, a 145-yard par 3.

## WEDGEWOOD SUPPER CLUB & GC

1200 E. Huron St. • P. O. Box 326 • Omro 54963 • 414/685-6161

**Directions:** Hwy. 41 to Hwy. 21, 8 miles west on Hwy. 21
**Course:** 9 holes/par 35/2,842 yards
**Fee:** $
**Amenities:** Remodeled dining room and new menu

Under new ownership, this relatively flat course has been spruced up with new sand traps and new grass. Fine greens and three significant water hazards make the course interesting.

## WESTHAVEN GC

1641 S. Main St. • Oshkosh 54901 • 414/233-4640

**Directions:** West of Hwy. 41 at 9th Avenue
**Course:** 18 holes/par 70/5,982 yards
**Fee:** $
**Amenities:** Pro shop; carts

This open course features some trees and large greens.

*The National Course at Fox Hills*

*Peninsula State Park in Door County*

## WEYMONT RUN CC

N 1061 Co. U • Weyauwega 54983 • 414/867-3412

**Directions:** One mile west of U.S. Hwy. 10, between Weyauwega and Fremont
**Course:** 9 holes/par 36/3,229 yards
**Fee:** $$

## WINAGAMIE GC

3501 Winagamie Dr. • Neenah 54956 • 414/757-5453

**Directions:** Six miles west of Hwy. 41 on Co. BB
**Course:** 18 holes/par 73/6,355 yards
**Fee:** $

Located in the countryside, this course offers sweeping views in all directions. Thousands of pine trees dominate this layout, in operation since 1962. Course improvements are being made every year on the recommendation of Packard Inc. The back nine recently has taken on a Scottish look, with the addition of rolling mounds.

## WINCHESTER HILLS GC

5310 Hwy. 110 • Larsen 54947 • 414/836-2476

**Directions:** Intersection of Hwys. 110 and 150 in Winchester
**Course:** 18 holes/par 65/4,347 yards
**Fee:** $

## WISCONSIN RIVER CC

705 West River Dr. • Stevens Point 54481 • 715/344-9152

**Directions:** Five miles southwest of Stevens Point on West River Drive
**Course:** 18 holes/par 72/6,665 yards
**Fee:** $$
**Amenities:** Golf shop; golf range; bar and grill

One thousand new trees have been recently added to this course, built in 1961.

## WOODSIDE CC

530 Erie Rd. • Green Bay 54311 • 414/468-5729

**Directions:** I-43 north to exit 183 (Mason Street), 1 1/2 miles east on Mason, then left on Erie Road two blocks
**Course:** 18 holes/par 71/6,002 yards
**Fee:** $
**Amenities:** Large banquet facilities

# Southwest Courses

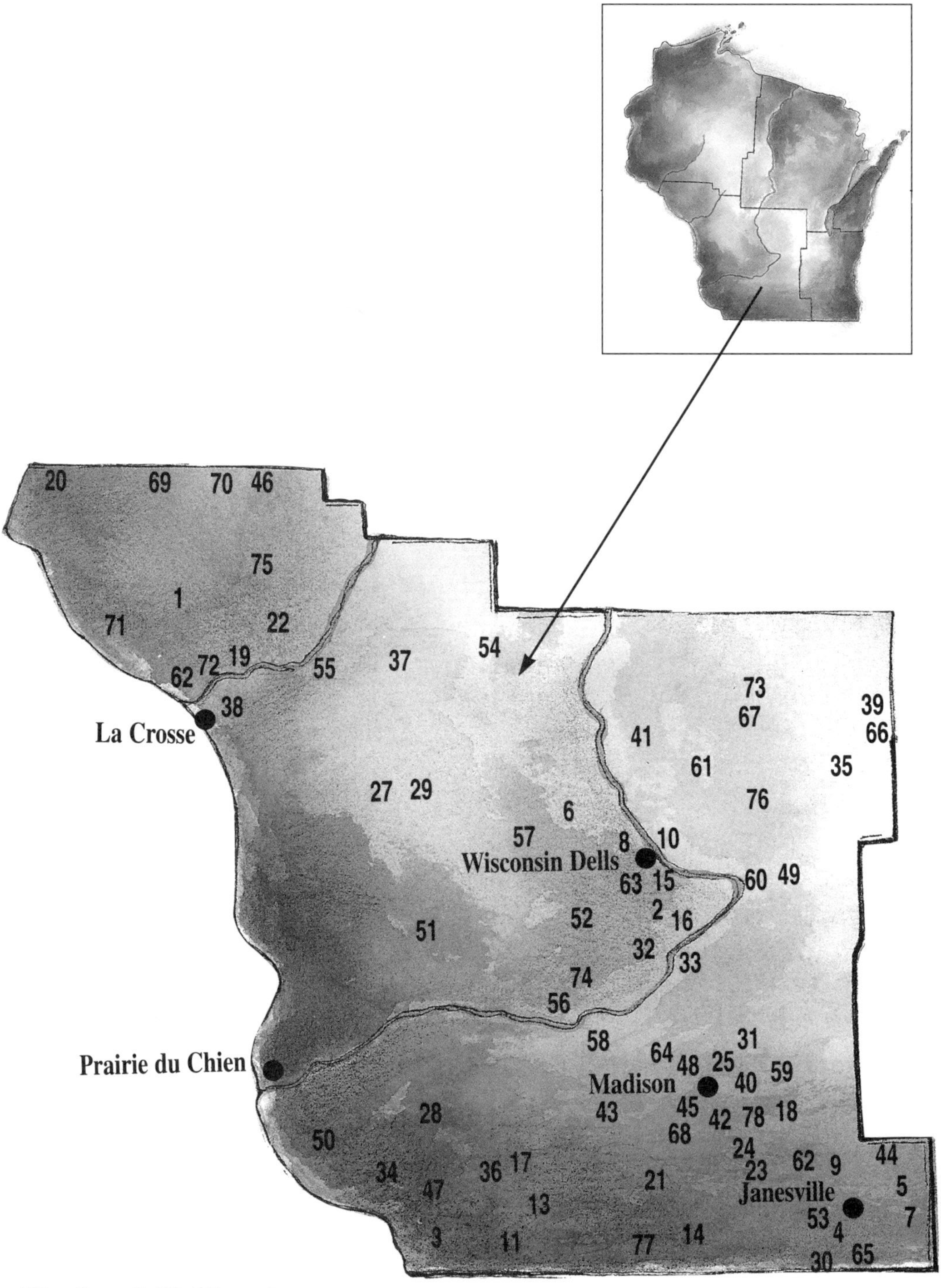

| No. | Page |
|---|---|
| 1 ARCADIA GOLF COURSE | 114 |
| 2 BARABOO COUNTRY CLUB | 114 |
| 3 BIRCHWOOD GOLF & DEVELOPMENT | 114 |
| 4 BLACKHAWK GOLF COURSE | 114 |
| 5 BONNY MEADE LINKS | 114 |
| 6 CASTLE ROCK GOLF COURSE | 115 |
| 7 CECELIA'S GOLF COURSE | 115 |
| 8 CHRISTMAS MOUNTAIN RESORT | 115 |
| 9 COACHMAN'S INN COUNTRY CLUB | 115 |
| 10 COLDWATER CANYON GOLF COURSE | 116 |
| 11 COLE ACRES GC & SUPPER CLUB | 116 |
| 12 COULEE GOLF BOWL | 116 |
| 13 DARLINGTON COUNTRY CLUB | 116 |
| 14 DECATUR LAKE COUNTRY CLUB | 117 |
| 15 DELL VIEW GOLF COURSE | 117 |
| 16 DEVIL'S HEAD LODGE | 118 |
| 17 DODGE POINT COUNTRY CLUB | 118 |
| 18 DOOR CREEK GOLF COURSE | 118 |
| 19 DRUGAN'S CASTLE MOUND | 118 |
| 20 DURAND GOLF COURSE | 118 |
| 21 EDELWEISS CHALET COUNTRY CLUB | 119 |
| 22 ETTRICK GOLF COURSE | 119 |
| 23 EVANSVILLE GOLF COURSE | 119 |
| 24 FOXBORO GOLF COURSE | 119 |
| 25 GLENWAY GOLF COURSE | 120 |
| 27 HIAWATHA GOLF COURSE | 120 |
| 28 HICKORY GROVE GOLF COURSE | 120 |
| 29 HOLIDAY LODGE GOLF RESORT | 121 |
| 30 KRUEGER MUNICIPAL GOLF COURSE | 121 |
| 31 LAKE WINDSOR GOLF COURSE | 121 |
| 32 LAKE WISCONSIN COUNTRY CLUB | 121 |
| 33 LAKELAND HILLS COUNTRY CLUB | 122 |
| 34 LANCASTER COUNTRY CLUB | 122 |
| 35 LAWSONIA | 122 |
| 36 LUDDEN LAKE GOLF COURSE | 122 |
| 37 MACDONALD'S RIVER BEND | 122 |
| 38 MAPLE GROVE COUNTRY CLUB | 123 |
| 39 MASCOUTIN GOLF CLUB | 123 |
| 40 MONONA GOLF COURSE | 123 |

| No. | Page |
|---|---|
| 41 MOUNDVIEW GOLF COURSE | 123 |
| 42 NINE SPRINGS GOLF COURSE | 124 |
| 43 NORSK GOLF BOWL | 124 |
| 44 OAK RIDGE GOLF COURSE | 124 |
| 45 ODANA HILLS GOLF COURSE | 124 |
| 46 OSSEO GOLF COURSE | 124 |
| 47 PLATTEVILLE GOLF & COUNTRY CLUB | 125 |
| 48 PLEASANT VIEW GOLF COURSE | 125 |
| 49 PORTAGE COUNTRY CLUB | 125 |
| 50 PRAIRIE DU CHIEN COUNTRY CLUB | 125 |
| 51 OUAIL RUN GOLF LINKS | 126 |
| 52 REEDSBURG COUNTRY CLUB | 126 |
| 53 RIVERSIDE GOLF COURSE | 126 |
| 54 SKYLINE GOLF COURSE | 126 |
| 55 SPARTA MUNICIPAL GOLF COURSE | 127 |
| 56 SPRING GREEN GOLF COURSE | 127 |
| 57 SPRING VALLEY GOLF COURSE | 127 |
| 58 SPRINGS GOLF CLUB RESORT, THE | 127 |
| 59 SUN PRAIRIE COUNTRY CLUB | 128 |
| 60 SWAN LAKE VILLAGE GOLF COURSE | 128 |
| 61 THAL ACRES LINKS & LANES | 128 |
| 62 TOWNE COUNTRY CLUB | 128 |
| 63 TRAPPERS TURN GOLF COURSE | 128 |
| 64 TUMBLEDOWN TRAILS GOLF COURSE | 129 |
| 65 TURTLE GREENS GOLF COURSE | 129 |
| 66 TUSCUMBIA GOLF COURSE | 129 |
| 67 TWO OAKS NORTH | 130 |
| 68 UNIVERSITY RIDGE GOLF COURSE | 130 |
| 69 VALLEY, THE | 130 |
| 70 VIKING SKYLINE GOLF | 131 |
| 71 WALNUT GROVE GOLF COURSE | 131 |
| 72 WALSH GOLF COURSE | 131 |
| 73 WAUSHARA COUNTRY CLUB | 131 |
| 74 WESTBROOK HILLS GOLF COURSE | 132 |
| 75 WHITEHALL GOLF COURSE | 132 |
| 76 WHITE LAKE COUNTRY CLUB | 133 |
| 77 WINDY ACRES GOLF COURSE | 133 |
| 78 YAHARA HILLS GOLF COURSE | 133 |

Southwest

## ARCADIA GC

Hwy. 93 • Arcadia 54612 • 608/323-3626

**Directions:** On Hwy. 93 between Eau Claire & La Crosse at the intersection of Hwy. 95
**Course:** 9 holes/par 35/2,751yards
**Fee:** $
**Amenities:** Driving range; pro shop; restaurant

This scenic course is surrounded by bluffs.

## BARABOO CC

1010 Lake St. • P. O. Box 383 • Baraboo 53913 • 608/356-8195 or 800/657-4981

**Directions:** Hwy. 12 from Madison to Hwy. 159 east to Hwy. 123 north
**Course:** 18 holes/par 72/6,578 yards
**Fee:** $$
**Amenities:** Pro shop; iron range; restaurant and bar

This rolling course offers nice views of the Baraboo Bluffs.

## BIRCHWOOD GOLF & DEVELOPMENT

3976 Eagle Point Rd. • P. O. Box 27 • Kieler 53812 • 608/748-4747

**Directions:** Off Hwy. 61/151 north at the end of Badger Road, or off Hwy. 61/151 south on Eagle Point Road
**Course:** 9 holes/par 36/3,327 yards
**Fee:** $

## BLACKHAWK GC

2100 Palmer Dr. • Janesville, WI 53545 • 608/757-3090

**Directions:** West of I-90 on Hwy. 11
**Course:** 9 holes/par 34/3,097 yards
**Fee:** $

## BONNY MEADE LINKS

Bowers Lake Road • Milton 53563 • 608/868-4353

**Directions:** From Janesville, four miles north on Hwy. 26
**Course:** 9 holes/par 36/3,090 yards
**Fee:** $
**Amenities:** Driving range

This Scottish links course offers a challenge to all golfers.

## CASTLE ROCK GC

P.O. Box 212 • Mauston 53948 • 608/847-4658 or 800/851-4853

**Directions:** I-90/94 to exit 69, Hwy. 82 west to Union Street (Co. Q), two miles north, then one-quarter mile west on Welch Prairie Road
**Course:** 18 holes/par 72/6,160 yards
**Fee:** $$
**Amenities:** Driving range; restaurant

Mature trees and abundant water characterize this picturesque course near I-90/94. Water can come into play on 15 holes, so accuracy is required. The new nine, added in 1991, is beginning to mature nicely, matching well with the original nine opened in 1974.

## CECELIA'S GC

2028 S. Emerald Grove Rd. • Janesville 53546 • 608/754-8550

**Directions:** Hwy. 14 seven miles east of Janesville to Emerald Grove, south one-half mile
**Course:** 9 holes/par 36/3,071 yards
**Fee:** $
**Amenities:** Driving range

## CHRISTMAS MOUNTAIN RESORT

S. 944 Christmas Mountain Rd. • Wisconsin Dells 53965 • 608/254-3971

**Directions:** I-90/94 to exit 87, left on Co. H four miles
**Course:** 18 holes/par 71/6,589 yards
**Fee:** $$$
**Amenities:** Year-round resort lodging; restaurant; full-service pro shop; tennis; clubhouse; swimming; skiing; special spring/fall and summer packages

This championship course provides a challenge for golfers of all levels.

## COACHMAN'S INN CC

984 Co. A • Edgerton 53534 • 608/884-8484 or 608/873-7900

**Directions:** Exit no. 156 from I-90, north on Hwy. 51
**Course:** 27 holes/par 71/6,184 yards, par 35/3,180 yards
**Fee:** $$
**Amenities:** Lodging; pool; restaurant; bar; pro shop; driving range

This course plays well and is easily accessible. It has a good mixture of wooded and open fairways. Unlimited golf package plans available.

## COLDWATER CANYON GC

4065 River Rd. • Wisconsin Dells 53965 • 608/254-8489

**Directions:** Two miles north of I-90/94 and Wisconsin Dells, Hwy. 13 east to River Road, then north along the Wisconsin River, adjacent to Chula Vista Resort
**Course:** 9 holes/par 33/2,444 yards
**Fee:** $$    Tee times required on weekends
**Amenities:** Clubhouse serving food and drinks

The course, designed by Chicago architect J.C. Wilson for pioneer Dells resort owner Clinton Berry, opened for play in June 1923 as Berry's Dells Golf Course. Built by horse-drawn equipment along Coldwater Canyon of the Upper Wisconsin River Dells, this traditional resort is best described as sporty and scenic. Hills, narrow fairways and small greens put a premium on accuracy. The canyon's beautiful white pines and hemlocks fill out the picture. Course record of 27 by amateur Hugh Byington of Hixton, Wis., has stood since 1939.

## COLE ACRES GC & SUPPER CLUB

Rural Route 1 • Cuba City 53807 • 608/744-2476

**Directions:** One mile east of Cuba City on Co. H and Co. J
**Course:** 9 holes/par 36/3,144 yards
**Fee:** $    Tee times required on weekends

Built in 1969 on a corn field, this challenging course and its young trees are beginning to mature. The course is characterized by rolling hills. A large pond comes into play on the ninth hole, but regulars say the toughest hole is the 440-yard, par-4 fourth hole. Two sets of tees provide a different look for the 18-hole golfer.

## COULEE GOLF BOWL

100 Greens Coulee Rd. • Onalaska 54650 • 608/781-1111

**Directions:** One-half mile north of I-90's exit 4, at the east end of Main Street in Onalaska
**Course:** 9 holes/par 36/3,060 yards
**Fee:** $

Built in 1962, this course lies at the head of one of the region's lovely valleys. It is a challenging course with small, contoured greens and narrow, tree-lined bluegrass fairways. Since its opening, new tee boxes, a pond and mounds have been added.

## DARLINGTON CC

17098 Country Club Rd. • Darlington 53530 • 608/776-3377

**Directions:** From Darlington, Hwy. 81 west to Platteville for 1 1/2

miles, then left one mile
**Course:** 9 holes/par 35/2,706 yards
**Fee:** $    Tee times required on weekends & holidays

This southwestern Wisconsin course is irrigated and is easily accessable on Mondays, Wednesdays and Fridays. It is open to members and guests only Tuesday and Thursday afternoons May 1st - Labor Day.

## DECATUR LAKE CC

N3941 Golf Course Rd. • Brodhead 53520 • 608/897-2777

**Directions:** North on Co. E from Brodhead for 1 1/2 miles, then left on Golf Course Road
**Course:** 18 holes/par 71/6,165 yards
**Fee:** $$
**Amenities:** Pro shop; bar; restaurant

New nine holes opening in June 1994.

## DELL VIEW GC

511 E. Adams St. • Wisconsin Dells 53965 • 608/253-GOLF

**Directions:** On Hwy. 12, one mile off I-90 in Lake Delton
**Course:** 18 holes/par 70/5,840 yards
**Fee:** $$
**Amenities:** Clubhouse bar and grill; pro shop; lighted driving range; complete practice facilities; hotel; indoor/outdoor pools

This sporty course, built in the 1920s, now has a new irrigation system to go along with the recent addition of more sand traps and a water hazard. Custom-tailored outings available.

*Trappers Turn in Wisconsin Dells*

## DEVIL'S HEAD LODGE

S6330 Bluff Rd. • Merrimac 53561 • 608/493-2251

**Directions:** Thirty miles north of Madison on I-90/94, exit 108 on Hwy. 78 for eight miles, right on Co. DL to Bluff Road
**Course:** 18 holes/par 73/6,725 yards
**Fee:** $$$   Tee times required, carts required until 4 p.m.

## DODGE POINT CC

Rural Route 3 • Mineral Point 53565 • 608/987-2814

**Directions:** Halfway between Mineral Point and Dodgeville on Hwy. 151
**Course:** 9 holes/par 35/2,950 yards
**Fee:** $$   Tee times required on weekends
**Amenities:** Pro shop; restaurant; driving range

This course, built in 1948, is lined with many large trees.

## DOOR CREEK GC

4321 Vilas Rd. • Cottage Grove 53527 • 608/839-5656

**Directions:** Between Cottage Grove and Madison off of Cottage Grove Road (BB)
**Course:** 18 holes/par 71/6,080 yards
**Fee:** $$
**Amenities:** Covered driving range; grill; full bar; pro shop

This course features uniquely contoured greens and nearly 4,000 recently planted trees. During the summer of '94, Door Creek will open its new Executive Course—a par-30 (three par 4s and six par 3s) 1,600-yard layout that will emphasize putting and the short game.

## DRUGAN'S CASTLE MOUND

W7665 Sylvester Rd. • Holmen 54636 • 608/526-3225

**Directions:** Seventeen miles north of La Crosse on Hwy. 53
**Course:** 18 holes/par 72/6,492 yards
**Fee:** $$
**Amenities:** Shower facilities; full-service supper club

Nestled in lush, green "coulee country," this 24-year-old course offers nice scenery and an interesting layout. It has undergone much revision since 1970, with only two of the original greens left. The newest: No. 7.

## DURAND GC

P. O. Box 129 • Durand 54736 • 715/672-8139

**Directions:** From Eau Claire, southwest on Hwy. 85 for 28 miles to Durand, then south one-half mile on 3rd Avenue West

**Course:** 9 holes/par 36/3,081 yards
**Fee:** $    Tee times required on weekends
**Amenities:** Pro shop; restaurant; full banquet facilities w/bar

## EDELWEISS CHALET CC

W4764 Edelweiss Rd. • New Glarus 53574 • 608/527-2315

**Directions:** South of New Glarus on Hwy. 69 (1 mile), left on Valley View Road, right on Edelweiss Road
**Course:** 18 holes/par 72/6,544 yards
**Fee:** $    Tee times required
**Amenities:** Driving range by summer '94

The front nine is tree-lined with huge greens, abundant bunkers and a gentle slope. The scenic back nine on this course has fewer bunkers and smaller, rolling greens.

## ETTRICK GC

310 N. Fairway • Ettrick 54627 • 608/525-6262

**Directions:** East of Hwy. 53 in Ettrick
**Course:** 9 holes/par 36/3,075 yards
**Fee:** $
**Amenities:** Pro shop; food; bar

## EVANSVILLE GC

Route 1, Cemetery Road • Evansville 53536 • 608/882-6524

**Directions:** Hwy. 14 between Madison and Janesville
**Course:** 18 holes/par 72/6,425 yards
**Fee:** $$
**Amenities:** Pro shop; restaurant; driving range

## FOXBORO GC

1020 Co. MM • Oregon 53575 • 608/835-7789

**Directions:** Just off Co. MM in Oregon
**Course:** 9 holes/par 36/3,622 yards
**Fee:** $$    Tee times required
**Amenities:** Clubhouse; bar; patio; pro shop

A sporty course, rolling but not hilly, with a few bunkers and little water would best describe the Foxboro Golf Club. The new nine will feature bentgrass fairways, tees and greens.

*And don't forget to look both ways. On the ninth hole at Glenway Golf Course in Madison, you can't tee off until the stoplight turns green.*

*Devil's Head Course in Merrimac*

## GLENWAY GC

3747 Speedway Rd. • Madison 53705 • 608/266-4737

**Directions:** Corner of Mineral Point and Speedway, north of Hwy. 12/18, on west side of city

**Course:** 9 holes/par 32/2,298 yards

**Fee:** $$

**Amenities:** Pro shop; food & beverages

Rolling hills and fully grown trees make for an interesting round.

## HIAWATHA GC

Route 1 • P. O. Box 287 • Tomah 54660 • 608/372-5589

**Directions:** West of Hwy. 12 on Hwy. 21 about one mile

**Course:** 9 holes/par 36/3,289 yards

**Fee:** $    Tee times required

A new nine is set to open at this course in the fall of '94.

## HICKORY GROVE GC

Rural Route 1 • P. O. Box 38 • Fennimore 53809 • 608/822-3314

**Directions:** On Hwy. 61, three miles north of Fennimore

**Course:** 9 holes/par 36/3,166 yards

**Fee:** $

**Amenities:** Driving range; locker rooms; bar/restaurant featuring Friday fish fry and Sunday brunch

This nicely landscaped course rolls over 80 acres of beautiful countryside. Flowered tee boxes enhance the course's 1,000 trees, shrubs and bushes. A pond borders much of the left side of one of the more challenging holes, the 472-yard, par-5 sixth hole.

## HOLIDAY LODGE GOLF RESORT & SUPPER CLUB

Route 2 • P. O. Box 298 • Tomah 54660 • 608/372-9314

**Directions:** Six miles east of Tomah in Wyeville, off I-90/94 exit 48 north on Co. PP
**Course:** 18 holes/par 71/6,010 yards
**Fee:** $    Tee times required on weekends
**Amenities:** RV campground; motel; lounge; supper club

This course has an island green on the par-3 17th hole. Nine holes were added in 1991 to the original nine, opened in 1969. Mature oaks, pines and sand traps complement the water hazards, which can come into play on at least 12 holes.

## KRUEGER MUNICIPAL GC

1611 Hackett • Beloit 53511 • 608/362-6503

**Directions:** On northwest side of Beloit, next to the municipal swimming pool
**Course:** 18 holes/par 70/6,103 yards
**Fee:** $$
**Amenities:** Pro shop; clubhouse; bar

This course has many trees to make for an interesting round of golf.

## LAKE WINDSOR CC

4628 Golf Rd. • Windsor 53598 • 608/255-6100

**Directions:** Four miles north of Madison, exit I-90/94 at Hwy. 19 to Lake Road (Co. CV), north to Golf Road
**Course:** 27 holes/par 35/2,956 yards, par 36/3,027 yards, par 36/3,201 yards
**Fee:** $$    Tee times required
**Amenities:** Large clubhouse

Just off I-94, this course has three distinct nines over low-lying terrain that provide variety for the mid-handicap golfer.

## LAKE WISCONSIN CC

N1076 Golf Rd. • Prairie du Sac 53578 • 608/643-2405

**Directions:** Across the river in Prairie du Sac, Hwy. 60 bridge east, then left on Golf Road
**Course:** 18 holes/par 70/5,860 yards
**Fee:** $$$
**Amenities:** Grill; banquet facilities; driving range; pro shop

Back nine offers an island tee and is on the water; the front nine is wonderfully wooded.

*Great Golf in Wisconsin*

## LAKELAND HILLS CC

Prospect Avenue • Lodi 53555 • 608/592-3757

**Directions:** At west end of city, west of I-94, between Madison and Wisconsin Dells
**Course:** 9 holes/par 35/2,751 yards
**Fee:** $$
**Amenities:** Cart rentals

A new No. 1 tee and No. 8 green are promised for 1994. Several new blacktopped cart paths have also been added.

## LANCASTER CC

East Lincoln Avenue • Lancaster 53813 • 608/723-4266

**Directions:** Off South Street to Madison, east on Lincoln
**Course:** 9 holes/par 36/3,126 yards
**Fee:** $

This nice course has hills, newer trees and narrow fairways.

## LAWSONIA

Hwy. 23 • Green Lake 54941 • 414/294-3320

**Directions:** Two miles west of Green Lake on Hwy. 23, Green Lake Conference Center
**Course:** 36 holes/par 72/6,764 yards, par 72/6,618 yards
**Fee:** $$$$ (Fee includes cart)
**Amenities:** Restaurant; conference room; locker rooms; one of largest pro shops in Wisconsin

## LUDDEN LAKE GC

Route 3 Box 100 • Mineral Point 53565 • 608/987-2888

**Directions:** Hwy. 151 to Hwy. 39 west to Co. QQ, about 1 1/2 miles from town
**Course:** 9 holes/par 34/2,500 yards
**Fee:** $
**Amenities:** Pro shop; lessons; equipment rentals; bar and grill, serving Friday night buffet; banquet room available; golf outings welcome

This scenic and sporty nine-hole course has rolling terrain and hilltop views of Ludden Lake.

## MACDONALD'S RIVER BEND

Route 2 • P. O. Box 70 • Melrose 54642 • 608/488-7291

**Directions:** On Hwy. 54, 21 miles from I-94 Black River Falls, 30 miles northeast of La Crosse

**Course:** 9 holes/par 35/2,888 yards
**Fee:** $
**Amenities:** Pro shop; food

Located on the scenic Black River, this course offers fantastic views.

# MAPLE GROVE CC

W4142 County B • West Salem 54669 • 608/786-1500

**Directions:** Fifteen minutes east of La Crosse on Co. B
**Course:** 18 holes/par 71/6,494 yards
**Fee:** $$    Tee times required
**Amenities:** New clubhouse; indoor pool; tennis courts; exercise facilities; pro shop; restaurant

This scenic, well-maintained course, built in 1929, mixes old-fashioned straight-away holes with some very interesting newer holes. One drive on a scenic par 4 is launched from a high bluff. Mature trees dot the course, which is situated on the hills just east of the Mississippi River Valley.

# MASCOUTIN GC

Co. A • Berlin 54923 • 414/361-2360

**Directions:** From Milwaukee, Hwy. 41 north to Hwy. 23 west to Green Lake, Hwy. 49 north seven miles, then left on Co. A
**Course:** 18 holes/par 72/6,821 yards
**Fee:** $$$    (Fee includes cart)
**Amenities:** PGA staff; pro shop; golf range; lessons; restaurant; dinner/golf packages

# MONONA GC

111 E. Dean Ave. • Madison 53716 • 608/266-4736

**Directions:** South of Madison, off I-90 on Hwy. 12/18, exit Monona Drive, two miles north
**Course:** 9 holes/par 36/3,157 yards
**Fee:** $$
**Amenities:** Pro shop; driving range; food & beverages

Small fast greens and plenty of traps provide a challenging round.

# MOUNDVIEW GC

1426 Co. J • Friendship 53934 • 608/339-3814

**Directions:** One mile west on Co. J in Friendship
**Course:** 9 holes/par 36/3,182 yards
**Fee:** $
**Amenities:** Pro shop; bar and restaurant; open seven days a week

## NINE SPRINGS GC

2201 Traceway Dr. • Madison 53713 • 608/271-5877

**Directions:** South of Hwy. 12/18 on Fish Hatchery Road
**Course:** 9 holes/par 30/1,650 yards
**Fee:** $
**Amenities:** Pro shop; snack bar; lessons

This course has water on seven of its nine holes, and its tees, greens and fairways are watered regularly.

## NORSK GOLF BOWL

Hwy. 18/151 Business East, 2755 Golf Bowl Rd. • Mt. Horeb 53572 • 608/437-3399

**Directions:** Business Hwy. 18/151, east edge of Mt. Horeb
**Course:** 9 holes/par 36/2,852 yards
**Fee:** $

This course is a hilly, well-drained layout atop a windswept knob on the edge of Wisconsin's driftless area. It is one of the first courses open every year.

## OAK RIDGE GC

Bowers Lake Road • Milton 53563 • 608/868-4353

**Directions:** From Janesville, four miles north on Hwy. 26
**Course:** 18 holes/par 70/6,049 yards
**Fee:** $$
**Amenities:** Pro shop; snack bar; bar

This course is sporty and well-manicured.

## ODANA HILLS GC

4635 Odana Rd. • Madison 53711 • 608/266-4724

**Directions:** Hwys. 12/18 to Midvale Boulevard exit, Midvale Boulevard to Odana Road, west two blocks
**Course:** 18 holes/par 72/6,486 yards
**Fee:** $$
**Amenities:** Driving range; putting green

This jewel of the Madison municipal layouts features gently rolling hills and interesting, well-designed hazards. Its moderate length makes it very playable for many skill levels.

## OSSEO GC

127 E. Park Ave. • Osseo 54758 • 715/597-3215

**Directions:** One mile south of I-94, two blocks off of Hwy. 53

**Course:** 9 holes/par 35/3,010 yards
**Fee:** $$

This old course, built prior to 1920, is a traditional layout on a relatively flat piece of land. It features two water holes, a variety of trees and a sprinkling of sand traps. The course offers a special discount rate on Mondays.

## PLATTEVILLE G & CC

6729 N. Water • Platteville 53818 • 608/348-3551

**Directions:** Hwy. 80 north off Hwy. 151
**Course:** 18 holes/par 71/6,014 yards
**Fee:** $$
**Amenities:** Pro shop; restaurant; bar

This well-maintained course offers fast greens and is very scenic.

## PLEASANT VIEW GC

4279 Pleasant View Rd. • Middleton 53562 • 608/831-6666

**Directions:** From Hwys. 12/18, exit Old Sauk Road west to Pleasant View Road, north to course
**Course:** 18 holes/par 72/6,436 yards
**Fee:** $
**Amenities:** Pro shop; driving range; restaurant

This 18-hole and nine-hole, par-3 course features lake and city views.

## PORTAGE CC

Route 1, East Hwy. 33 • Portage 53901 • 608/742-5121

**Directions:** Five miles east of Portage on Hwy. 33
**Course:** 18 holes/par 72/6,300 yards
**Fee:** $$
**Amenities:** Restaurant

Fairways lined with large oak and pine trees make this course, which overlooks beautiful Swan Lake, very tight.

## PRAIRIE DU CHIEN CC

Hwy. 18 • P. O. Box 11 • Prairie du Chien 53821 • 608/326-6707

**Directions:** Two miles south of Prairie du Chien on Hwy. 18/35
**Course:** 18 holes/par 71/6,240 yards
**Fee:** $$
**Amenities:** Pro shop; motorized carts; driving range; lessons; bar & grill facilities

New nine holes opened fall 1993. The course offers scenic views and challenging golf surrounded by the beautiful bluffs along the Wisconsin and Mississippi rivers.

*Great Golf in Wisconsin*

## QUAIL RUN GL

Co. Y • Richland Center 53581 • 608/647-3117

**Directions:** Hwy. 14 to Seminary Street in Richland Center, then left on Co. Y
**Course:** 9 holes/par 35/2,603 yards
**Fee:** $
**Amenities:** Bar & restaurant; pro shop

Newly watered fairways.

## REEDSBURG CC

P.O. Box 125 • Reedsburg 53959 • 608/524-6000

**Directions:** West of I-90/94 on Hwy. 23/33
**Course:** 18 holes/par 72/6,283 yards
**Fee:** $$$   Tee times required
**Amenities:** Practice facilities

This revamped course, close to the Wisconsin Dells attractions, has been getting a lot of attention from golfers since its 1977 redesign into a championship layout by then-partners Ken Killian and Dick Nugent. The redesign created 13 new holes, offering tree-lined fairways and views of bluffs. Six water crossings and fast bentgrass greens add to the challenge.

## RIVERSIDE GC

2100 Golf Course Rd. • Janesville 53545 • 608/757-3080

**Directions:** Northwest of Janesville on Co. E (Washington Street)
**Course:** 18 holes/par 72/6,508 yards
**Fee:** $$
**Amenities:** Drinks and sandwiches

This beautifully landscaped course lies on the hilly terrace above the Rock River. Built in 1924, it maintains an old-course feel. It features tough par 4s.

## SKYLINE GC

P.O. Box 8 • Black River Falls 54615 • 715/284-2613

**Directions:** I-94 to Main Street (Hwy. 54), right on 10th Street, then left on Golf Road
**Course:** 18 holes/par 72/6,371 yards
**Fee:** $$   Tee times required

There are two distinct nine-hole courses here. The front nine, built in 1957, is set among beautiful rolling hills. The back nine, built in 1989, is a well-trapped layout cut from stands of white pines and oaks. A bubbling brook adds beauty and challenge to the newer nine.

## SPARTA MUNICIPAL GC

1210 E. Montgomery St. • Sparta 54656 • 608/269-3022

**Directions:** Two blocks off of Hwy. 21 on Montgomery Street
**Course:** 18 holes/par 72/6,544 yards
**Fee:** $$
**Amenities:** Restaurant; bar; pro shop

One of the Wisconsin Golf Association's top ten municipal courses.

## SPRING GREEN GC

P.O. Box 247 • Spring Green 53588
No telephone at course; no tee times needed

**Directions:** Hwy. 23 in Spring Green
**Course:** 9 holes/par 33/2,426 yards
**Fee:** $

This course, founded in 1925, is short (the longest hole is 380 yards) but very challenging. Regulars say the par-3 fifth hole, at 217 yards, is as difficult a par 3 as you'll find anywhere. A new irrigation system should improve turf quality.

## SPRING VALLEY GC

P.O. Box 78 • Union Center 53962 • 608/462-8691

**Directions:** Hwys. 80/82 and 83, south of Co. W
**Course:** 9 holes/par 36/2,921 yards
**Fee:** $$

## THE SPRINGS GOLF CLUB RESORT

5857 Golf Course Rd. • Spring Green 53588 • 608/588-7707 or 800/626-3085

**Directions:** Hwy. 14 to Hwy. 23, southeast on Co. C, then south on Golf Course Road
**Course:** 27 holes/par 71/6,446 yards, par 35/3,010 yards
**Fee:** $$$
**Amenities:** Full-service resort with suites; pro shop; restaurant; fitness/aquatics center; tennis; racquetball; volleyball; croquet; trails for walking, biking, skiing

*Now that's a mighty slow train.* The green on the 161-yard, par-3 seventh hole of the Links course at Lawsonia in Green Lake gets its elevation from a boxcar buried beneath it.

## SUN PRAIRIE CC

Happy Valley Road • Sun Prairie 53950 • 608/837-6211

**Directions:** Hwy 151 exit, Co. C, 2 miles north to Happy Valley Road, right 2 miles
**Course:** 18 holes/par 72/6,800 yards
**Fee:** $
**Amenities:** Bar; driving range; pro shop; banquet facilities

This course offers very large greens to test your putting.

## SWAN LAKE VILLAGE GC

W7665 Hwy. 33 • Portage 53901 • 608/742-2181

**Directions:** On Hwy. 33, four miles east of Portage
**Course:** 9 holes/par 35/2,983 yards
**Fee:** $$
**Amenities:** Clubhouse; food & beverages

This is a challenging, well-groomed course, easily walked.

## THAL ACRES LINKS & LANES

Route 2 • P. O. Box 4 • Westfield 53964 • 608/296-2850

**Directions:** Hwy. 51 to exit 113 at Westfield, then Co. J west to Co. M, south two miles
**Course:** 18 holes/par 70/5,588 yards
**Fee:** $$
**Amenities:** Driving range; bowling center; banquet facilities; complete pro shop; clubhouse

Established in 1963, this course is nestled in the beautiful central Wisconsin countryside. Nine holes were added in 1977. Five lakes and tree-lined fairways round out the setting.

## TOWNE CC

115 Jensen St. • P.O. Box 128 • Edgerton 53534 • 608/884-4231

**Directions:** In Edgerton off of Hwy. 51 by A&W
**Course:** 9 holes/par 34/2,696 yards
**Fee:** $$

This hilly course with lots of trees was built in 1929.

## TRAPPERS TURN GC

625 Trappers Turn Dr. • P.O. Box 176 • Wisconsin Dells 53965 • 608/253-7000

**Directions:** Take I-90/94 exit 85, turn east on Hwy. 12/16. Go 1 1/2 miles to Trappers Turn.

**Course:** 18 holes/par 72/6,051 yards
**Fee:** $$$ (includes cart)   Tee times required, carts required until 3 p.m.
**Amenities:** Clubhouse; dining room; bar and grill; scenic veranda with view; pro shop; locker rooms

This course, designed by two-time U.S. Open champion Andy North and award-winning architect Roger Packard, offers a refreshing new style of golf, combining beauty, drama and challenge with shot value, variety and playability.

## TUMBLEDOWN TRAILS GC

7671 W. Mineral Point Rd. • Verona 53593 • 608/833-2301

**Directions:** 3 1/2 miles west of Hwys. 12/14 on Mineral Point Road
**Course:** 9 holes/par 36/3,181 yards
**Fee:** $

## TURTLE GREENS GC

7901 S. Schroeder Road • Beloit 53511 • 608/676-4334

**Directions:** East of Beloit off Co. X
**Course:** 9 holes/par 34/2,400 yards
**Fee:** $
**Amenities:** Pro shop

## TUSCUMBIA GC

Illinois Avenue, Box 473 • Green Lake 54941 • 414/294-3240

**Directions:** South of Hwy. 23 in Green Lake
**Course:** 18 holes/par 71/6,301 yards
**Fee:** $$
**Amenities:** Pro shop; driving range; grill & bar

Narrow fairways and small greens are the characteristics of Tuscumbia.

*The course at University Ridge in Verona*

*The golf course at Lawsonia*

## TWO OAKS NORTH

P.O. Box 1000 • Wautoma 54970 • 414/787-7132

**Directions:** Hwy. 73 south out of Wautoma, then two miles on Co. F

**Course:** 9 holes/par 36/3,250 yards

**Fee:** $$

**Amenities:** Driving range; full-service pro shop; fully equipped bar; sandwiches

Built in 1990, this course is set amid oaks and pines. Two water hazards add to the beauty. The course is challenging yet very playable.

## UNIVERSITY RIDGE GC

University of Wisconsin Golf Course
7120 County Trunk PD • Verona 53593 • 608/845-7700

**Directions:** From Mineral Point Road, Co. M south to Co. PD, then west one-half mile

**Course:** 18 holes/par 72/6,825 yards

**Fee:** $$$$    Cart required on weekends

**Amenities:** Driving range; golf shop; refreshment area; putting greens

*Golf Digest* rates this course No. 3 in Wisconsin.

## THE VALLEY

Route 1, Hwy. 37 North • Mondovi 54755 • 715/926-4913

**Directions:** One mile north of Mondovi on Hwy. 37 north, about 16 miles south of Eau Claire off I-94 Mondovi exit

**Course:** 9 holes/par 35/2,985 yards
**Fee:** $
**Amenities:** Pro shop; bar; restaurant; bowling alley

# VIKING SKYLINE GOLF

Hwy. 10 East • P. O. Box 386 • Strum 54770 • 715/695-3306

**Directions:** I-94 south to Osseo exit, then Hwy. 10 west approximately eight miles
**Course:** 9 holes/par 36/3,030 yards
**Fee:** $    Tee times required on weekends
**Amenities:** Driving range; full-service bar and restaurant; pro shop

Until the mid-1980s, this course had sand greens, but now the greens are large and made of real grass. The relatively flat layout has many pines and a lot of water (five holes include or touch water). The feature hole is No. 6, a 135-yard par 3. Here the golfer must hit over water and between two willow trees.

# WALNUT GROVE GC

W1440 Co. O • Cochrane 54622 • 608/248-2800

**Directions:** Hwy. 35 in Cochrane
**Course:** 9 holes/par 35/3,036 yards
**Fee:** $    Tee times required
**Amenities:** Driving range

This relatively new course (opened in 1979) is built at the mouth of a valley amid the scenic bluffs along the Mississippi River. Fall is an especially nice time of year to play the course because of the contrast between the many evergreens and the beautifully colored hillsides.

# WALSH GC

4203 Co. B • La Crosse 54601 • 608/781-0838

**Directions:** South of Valley View Mall, one-quarter mile on Co. B
**Course:** 9 holes/par 32/2,145 yards
**Fee:** $
**Amenities:** Pro shop; practice green; miniature golf; bar

# WAUSHARA CC

Hillside Drive • Wautoma 54982 • 414/787-4649

**Directions:** Just east of Wautoma at the junction of Hwys. 21 and 73
**Course:** 18 holes/par 72/5,737 yards
**Fee:** $$

Nine new holes, through the woods and over water, are being added to this course. The older 18 is sometimes hilly, sometimes wooded. One hole overlooks Big Silver Lake, where the fall views are breathtaking.

*Great Golf in Wisconsin*

*Lake Windsor Country Club*

## WESTBROOK HILLS GC

American Legion Drive • Plain 53577 • 608/546-4432

**Directions:** On Hwy. 23, seven miles north of junction of Hwys. 14 and 23
**Course:** 9 holes/par 33/2,463 yards
**Fee:** Unavailable at time of printing

## WHITEHALL GC

West and Creamery Streets • Whitehall 54773 • 715/538-4800

**Directions:** From Hwy. 53, west on Blair Street four blocks, or from Hwy. 121, north on West Street four blocks
**Course:** 9 holes/par 35/3,101 yards
**Fee:** $
**Amenities:** Food & beverages

Rolling terrain, featuring a tough starting hole.

## WHITE LAKE CC

Rural Route 2 • P. O. Box 274 • Montello 53949 • 608/297-2255

**Directions:** Off Hwy. 23, between Montello and Princeton
**Course:** 9 holes/par 36/3,258 yards
**Fee:** $
**Amenities:** Vacation homes; cottages; motel and apartments; two cocktail lounges; restaurant and supper club; pro shop; driving range; spring and fall golf packages; swimming; fishing; skiing; sailing on White Lake

## WINDY ACRES GC

N1005 Co. K • Monroe 53566 • 608/325-3240

**Directions:** Five miles south of Monroe on Co. K
**Course:** 9 holes/par 36/2,866 yards
**Fee:** $

This course was built in 1958.

## YAHARA HILLS GC

6701 E. Broadway • Madison 53704 • 608/838-3126

**Directions:** Hwys. 12/18, one mile east of I-90
**Course:** 36 holes/par 72/6,841 yards, par 72/6,968 yards
**Fee:** $$

# Southeast Courses

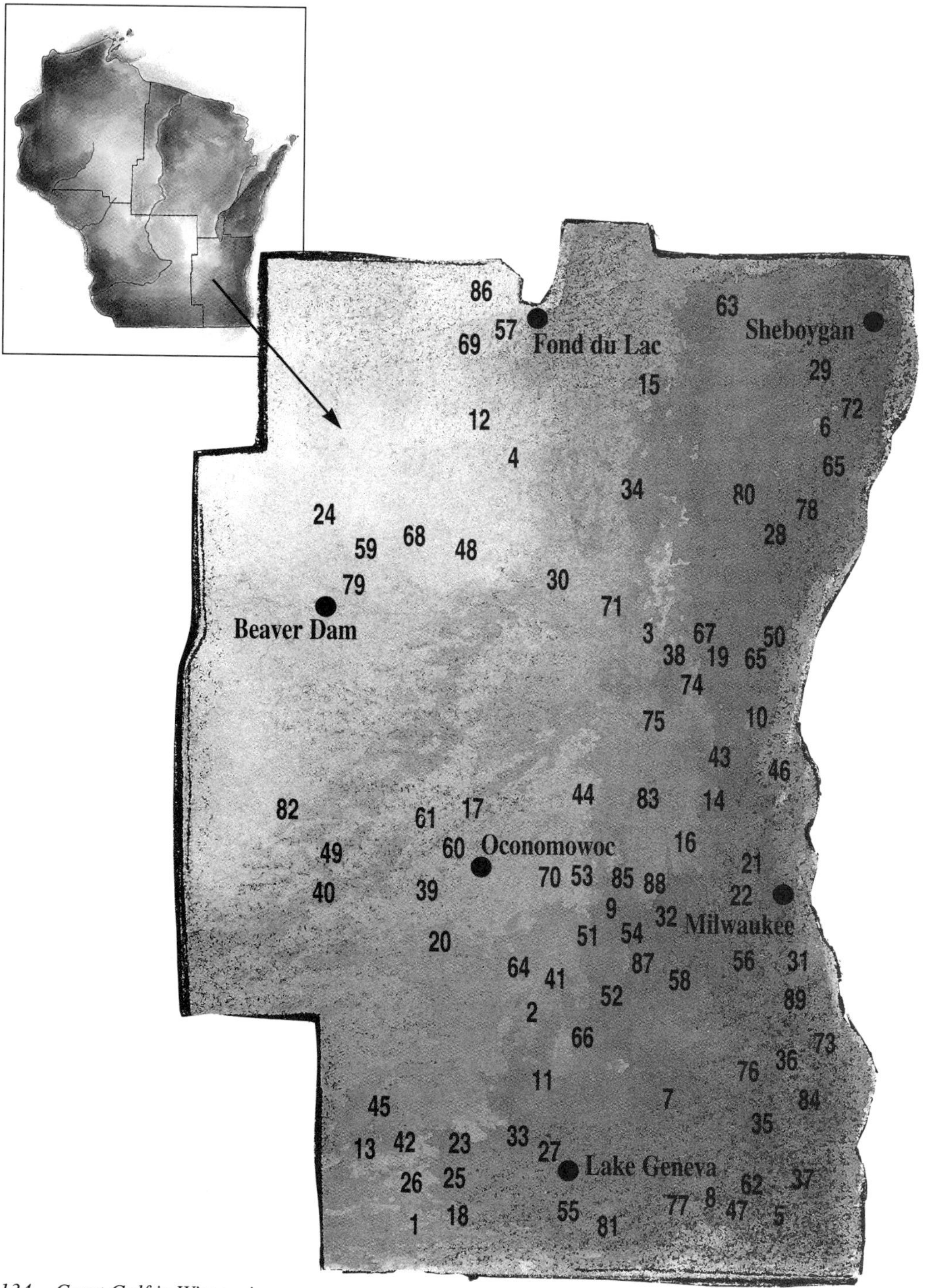

| No. | Page |
|---|---|
| 1 ABBEY SPRINGS GOLF COURSE | 136 |
| 2 ALPINE VALLEY RESORT | 136 |
| 3 ARROWHEAD SPRINGS | 136 |
| 4 AUBURN BLUFF GOLF COURSE | 136 |
| 5 BIG OAKS GOLF COURSE | 136 |
| 6 BLACKWOLF RUN | 136 |
| 7 BRIGHTON DALE LINKS | 137 |
| 8 BRISTOL OAKS COUNTRY CLUB | 137 |
| 9 BROOKFIELD HILLS GOLF COURSE | 137 |
| 10 BROWN DEER GOLF COURSE | 138 |
| 11 BROWN'S LAKE GOLF COURSE | 138 |
| 12 CAMELOT COUNTRY CLUB | 138 |
| 13 COUNTRY CLUB ESTATES | 138 |
| 14 COUNTRY CLUB OF WISCONSIN | 138 |
| 15 CRYSTAL LAKE GOLF COURSE | 139 |
| 16 CURRIE PARK GOLF COURSE | 139 |
| 17 DEERTRAK GOLF COURSE | 139 |
| 18 DELBROOK GOLF COURSE | 139 |
| 19 DRETZKA PARK GOLF COURSE | 139 |
| 20 EAGLE SPRINGS GOLF RESORT | 140 |
| 21 EDGEWATER | 140 |
| 22 EDGEWOOD GOLF COURSE | 140 |
| 23 EVERGREEN COUNTRY CLUB | 140 |
| 24 FOX LAKE GOLF COURSE | 140 |
| 25 GENEVA NATIONAL GOLF CLUB | 141 |
| 26 GEORGE WILLIAMS COLLEGE GOLF COURSE | 141 |
| 27 GRAND GENEVA RESORT & SPA | 141 |
| 28 GRANT PARK GOLF COURSE | 141 |
| 29 GREENFIELD PARK GOLF COURSE | 142 |
| 30 HARTFORD GOLF COURSE | 142 |
| 31 HAWTHORNE HILLS GOLF COURSE | 142 |
| 32 HEARTLAND HILLS GOLF COURSE | 142 |
| 33 HILLMOOR GOLF COURSE | 142 |
| 34 HON-E-KOR COUNTRY CLUB | 143 |
| 35 IVES GROVE GOLF LINKS | 143 |
| 36 JOHNSON PARK GOLF COURSE | 144 |
| 37 KENOSHA MUNICIPAL | 144 |
| 38 KETTLE HILLS GOLF COURSE | 144 |
| 39 KETTLE MORAINE GOLF COURSE | 145 |
| 40 KOSHKONONG MOUNDS COUNTRY CLUB | 145 |
| 41 LAKE BEULAH COUNTRY CLUB | 145 |
| 42 LAKE LAWN LODGE GOLF COURSE | 145 |
| 43 LAKE PARK GOLF COURSE | 146 |
| 44 LAKESIDE GOLF COURSE | 146 |
| 45 LAUDERDALE LAKES COUNTRY CLUB | 146 |
| 46 LINCOLN PARK GOLF COURSE | 146 |
| 47 MAPLECREST COUNTRY CLUB | 146 |
| 48 MAYVILLE GOLF COURSE | 146 |
| 49 MEADOW SPRINGS GOLF COURSE | 147 |
| 50 MEE-KWON PARK GOLF COURSE | 147 |
| 51 MOOR DOWNS GOLF COURSE | 147 |
| 52 MUSKEGO LAKES COUNTRY CLUB | 148 |
| 53 NAGA-WAUKEE GOLF COURSE | 148 |
| 54 NEW BERLIN HILLS GOLF COURSE | 148 |
| 55 NIPPERSINK COUNTRY CLUB | 148 |
| 56 OAK HILLS GOLF COURSE | 148 |
| 57 OAKGREEN GOLF COURSE & DRIVING RANGE | 149 |
| 58 OAKWOOD GOLF COURSE | 149 |
| 59 OLD HICKORY COUNTRY CLUB | 149 |
| 60 OLYMPIA RESORT GOLF COURSE | 150 |
| 61 PAGANICA GOLF COURSE | 150 |
| 62 PETRIFYING SPRINGS GOLF COURSE | 150 |
| 63 QUIT-QUI-OC GOLF COURSE | 150 |
| 64 RAINBOW SPRINGS GOLF COURSE | 150 |
| 65 RIVERDALE COUNTRY CLUB | 151 |
| 66 RIVERMOOR COUNTRY CLUB | 151 |
| 67 RIVERSBEND GOLF COURSE | 152 |
| 68 ROCK RIVER HILLS | 152 |
| 69 ROLLING MEADOWS GOLF COURSE | 152 |
| 70 ST. JOHN'S MILITARY ACADEMY | 152 |
| 71 SCENIC VIEW COUNTRY CLUB | 152 |
| 72 SHEBOYGAN TOWN & COUNTRY | 153 |
| 73 SHOOP PARK GOLF COURSE | 153 |
| 74 SILVER SPRING COUNTRY CLUB | 153 |
| 75 SONGBIRD HILLS GOLF COURSE | 154 |
| 76 SOUTH HILLS COUNTRY CLUB | 154 |
| 77 SPRING VALLEY COUNTRY CLUB | 154 |
| 78 SQUIRES GOLF COURSE, THE | 154 |
| 79 SUNSET HILLS GOLF & SUPPER CLUB | 154 |
| 80 TRENTON VIEW | 155 |
| 81 TWIN LAKES COUNTRY CLUB | 155 |
| 82 TYRANENA GOLF COURSE | 155 |
| 83 WANAKI GOLF COURSE | 155 |
| 84 WASHINGTON PARK GOLF COURSE | 155 |
| 85 WESTERN LAKES GOLF COURSE | 156 |
| 86 WHISPERING SPRINGS | 156 |
| 87 WHITNALL GOLF COURSE | 156 |
| 88 WILLOW RUN GOLF COURSE | 157 |
| 89 WOODLAND GOLF COURSE | 157 |

*Southeast*

## ABBEY SPRINGS GC

South Shore Drive • Fontana 53125 • 414/275-6113

**Directions:** 1 1/2 miles east of Hwy. 67 on South Shore Drive (Fontana Boulevard)
**Course:** 18 holes/par 72/6,466 yards
**Fee:** $$$$    Carts required (Fee includes cart)

## ALPINE VALLEY RESORT

Co. D • East Troy 53120 • 414/642-7374 or 800/433-5330

**Directions:** 4 1/2 miles south of East Troy on Co. D
**Course:** 27 holes/par 36/3,084 yards, par 35/2,833 yards, par 36/2,764 yards
**Fee:** $$

## ARROWHEAD SPRINGS

3468 Hwy. 167 • Richfield 53076 • 414/628-2298

**Directions:** 1 1/4 miles west of. Hwy. 41 on Hwy. 167
**Course:** 9 holes/par 34/2,680 yards
**Fee:** $    Tee times required
**Amenities:** Pro shop

## AUBURN BLUFF GC

1771 E. River Rd. • Campbellsport 53010 • 414/533-4311

**Directions:** 1 mile east of Campbellsport on Hwy. 67
**Course:** 9 holes/par 36/2,908 yards
**Fee:** $

## BIG OAKS GC

6117 123rd St. • Pleasant Prairie 53140 • 414/694-4200

**Directions:** One-half mile north of Russell Road on Green Bay Road
**Course:** 18 holes/par 72/6,071 yards
**Fee:** $$
**Amenities:** Snack bar

Small and elevated greens provide challenge and test your short game.

## BLACKWOLF RUN

1111 W. Riverside Dr. • Kohler 53044 • 414/457-4446

**Directions:** I-94 west to Milwaukee, then I-43 north to exit 126, west onto Hwy. 23, exit Co. Y (Kohler), south into Kohler
**Course:** 36 holes/par 72/6,991 yards, par 72/7,142 yards

*136    Great Golf in Wisconsin*

**Fee:** $$$$   Tee times required
**Amenities:** Pro shop; restaurant; bar; driving range; locker room; meeting & banquet facilities; lesson program

Designed by Pete Dye, these two 18-hole championship courses rediscover the challenge and strategy of the grand tradition. One of six greatest golf experiences in North America and one of the 25 best values, as rated by 10,000 readers of *Golf Digest*.

## BRIGHTON DALE LINKS

830 248th Ave. • Kansasville 53139 • 414/878-1440

**Directions:** On Hwy. 75, 10 miles west of I-94 exit Hwy. 142
**Course:** 45 holes/par 72/6,977 yards, par 72/6,687 yards, par 36/3,505 yards
**Fee:** $   Tee times required
**Amenities:** Pro shop; concessions; driving range

## BRISTOL OAKS CC

16801 75th St. • Bristol 53104 • 414/857-2302

**Directions:** Two miles west of I-94 on Hwy. 50
**Course:** 18 holes/par 72/6,187 yards
**Fee:** $$

Cart is required for play on weekends and holidays for tee times between 7:29 a.m. and 9:52 a.m.

## BROOKFIELD HILLS GC

16075 Pinehurst Dr. • Brookfield 53005 • 414/782-0885

**Directions:** Off Moorland Road, just south of I-94
**Course:** 18 holes/par 62/4,654 yards
**Fee:** $   Reservations required up to seven days in advance
**Amenities:** Cocktail lounge; pro shop

*Old Hickory Country Club in Beaver Dam*

## BROWN DEER GC

7835 N. Brown Deer Rd. • Milwaukee 53209 • 414/352-8080

**Directions:** Exit I-43, west on Good Hope to Range Line Road, then follow signs
**Course:** 18 holes/par 71/6,763 yards
**Fee:** $$$
**Amenities:** Golf shop and clubhouse

## BROWN'S LAKE GC

3110 S. Browns Lake Dr. • Burlington 53105 • 414/763-6065

**Directions:** On the Fox River, 1 1/2 miles south of Hwy. 36 on Co. W
**Course:** 18 holes/par 72/6,415 yards
**Fee:** $$
**Amenities:** Restaurant; bar; pro shop; clubhouse

## CAMELOT CC

Hwy. 67 East • Lomira 53048 • 414/269-4949

**Directions:** In Lomira, 30 miles north of Milwaukee on Hwy. 67, one mile east of Hwy. 41
**Course:** 18 holes/par 71/6,046 yards
**Fee:** $$
**Amenities:** Clubhouse; conference room; dining room; bar

This course is fully irrigated, with mature trees, manicured fairways, challenging greens and elevated tees enclosed in the picturesque countryside of the Northern Kettle Moraine State Forest.

## COUNTRY CLUB ESTATES

Shabbona Drive • Fontana 53125 • 414/275-3705

**Directions:** 1/2 mile from the Abbey Resort in Fontana
**Course:** 9 holes/par 35/2,920 yards
**Fee:** $$
**Amenities:** Limited pro shop; snack bar

This course was designed more than 60 years ago.

## COUNTRY CLUB OF WISCONSIN

2241 Highway W • Grafton 53024 • 414/375-2444

**Directions:** Twenty miles north of downtown Milwaukee just off I-43
**Course:** 18 holes/par 72/7,108 yards
**Fee:** $$$
**Amenities:** Practice range; clubhouse; restaurant; bar; PGA professional available

This course features rolling, wooded terrain with a championship layout, bentgrass fairways, tees and greens. It will host the 1995 Wisconsin PGA Championship.

## CRYSTAL LAKE GC

W6603 Co. C • Plymouth 53073 • 414/892-4834

**Directions**: Five miles north of Plymouth on Co. C, north on C from Hwy. 23
**Course:** 18 holes/par 65/4,300 yards
**Fee:** $

## CURRIE PARK GC

3535 N. Mayfair Rd. • Wauwatosa 53222 • 414/453-7030

**Directions:** Corner of Hwy. 100 and Capitol Drive
**Course:** 18 holes/par 70/6,334 yards
**Fee:** $$
**Amenities:** Pro shop; restaurant

This scenic 18-hole, watered course is very wooded.

## DEERTRAK GC

W930 Co. O • Oconomowoc 53066 • 414/474-4444

**Directions:** Hwy. 16 to Co. P, north to Co. O, east.
**Course:** 18 holes/par 72/6,262 yards
**Fee:** $$$

## DELBROOK GC

Delavan 53115 • 414/728-3966

**Directions:** Six blocks south on 2nd Street in Delavan
**Course:** 18 holes/par 72/6,516 yards
**Fee:** $$

## DRETZKA PARK GC

12020 W. Bradley Rd. • Milwaukee 53224 • 414/354-7300

**Directions:** Hwy. 41/45 north to Hwy. 145, then about one mile north on Hwy. 145, follow signs
**Course:** 18 holes/par 71/6,832 yards
**Fee:** $$

 ***And leave the parking to us.*** *Valet services are par for the course at the Geneva National Golf Club in Lake Geneva.*

## EAGLE SPRINGS GOLF RESORT

W352 S10355 Tuohy Rd. • Eagle 53119 • 414/594-2462

**Directions:** Take I-43 to Hwy. 83, Mukwonago exit, north on Hwy. 83, then 6 1/2 miles west on Hwy. 99
**Course:** 9 holes/par 35/2,814 yards
**Fee:** $$   Tee times required

This is a challenging course sculpted out of rolling hills and striking glacial features. The century-old course lies on the shores of Eagle Springs Lake, where sandhill cranes come to nest. One of the special holes is the par-3, 134-yard second hole, where golfers hit to a green perched atop a volcanolike hill.

## EDGEWATER

1762 E. Cedar Creek Rd. • Grafton  53024 • 414/377-1230

**Directions:**  I-43 to Hwy. 60 (exit 92), west to Co. O, right turn, go 1 1/4 mile to Cedar Creek Road
**Course**: 9 holes/par 36/3,259 yards
**Fee:** $
**Amenities:**  Restaurant; bar

This 30-year-old course is well-developed and walkable, enough challenge for golfers of all levels.

## EDGEWOOD GC

W240 S9950 Castle Rd. • Big Bend 53103 • 414/662-3110

**Directions:** Hwy. 43 west to Big Bend exit, then about 1 1/2 miles west on Co. L
**Course:** 27 holes/par 36/3,211 yards, par 36/3,225 yards, par 36/3,130 yards
**Fee:** $$

## EVERGREEN CC

Hwys. 12 & 67 North • Elkhorn 53121 • 414/723-5722

**Directions:** Three miles north of Elkhorn on Hwys. 12 and 67
**Course:** 18 holes/par 72/6,590 yards
**Fee:** $$$   Tee times recommended
**Amenities:** Driving range; lessons

This  championship course has all the elements of an excellent round of golf.

## FOX LAKE GC

N. 10500 Indian Point Rd. • Fox Lake 53933 • 414/928-2508

**Directions:** Just off of Hwy. 33 in Dodge County

**Course:** 9 holes/par 36/3,050 yards
**Fee:** $$

This course was built in 1922.

## GENEVA NATIONAL GC

1221 Geneva National Ave. South • Lake Geneva 53147 • 414/245-7010

**Directions:** Four miles west of Lake Geneva on Hwy. 50, or one-half mile east of intersection of Hwys. 50 and 67
**Course:** 36 holes/par 72/7,171 yards, par 72/7,120 yards
**Fee:** $$$$    Tee time and cart required
**Amenities:** Pro shop; driving range; lessons; golf school; locker room; club storage; valet parking; banquet facilities

## GEORGE WILLIAMS COLLEGE GC

350 Constance Blvd. • Williams Bay 53191 • 414/245-5531

**Directions:** Hwy. 50 west to Hwy. 67
**Course:** 18 holes/par 67/5,066 yards
**Fee:** $$
**Amenities:** Snack bar; pro shop

This picturesque course dates back to the turn of the century. It is well-developed and wooded.

## GRAND GENEVA RESORT & SPA

Hwy. 50 East • Lake Geneva 53147 • 414/248-8811

**Directions:** Hwy 50 east of Lake Geneva
**Course:** 36 holes/par 72/7,258 yards, par 71/6,742 yards
**Fee:** $$$$

## GRANT PARK GC

100 Hawthorne Ave. • South Milwaukee 53172 • 414/762-4646

**Directions:** I-94 to College Avenue exit east, five miles to Lake Drive, then south 1 1/2 miles to Hawthorne Avenue, east one-half mile
**Course:** 18 holes/par 67/5,174 yards
**Fee:** $$
**Amenities:** Night golf

 ***In memory of Hugh.*** *The Playboy bunnies are long gone from Grand Geneva Resort & Spa in Lake Geneva, but the "bunny dormitories" remain, along the left side of the Brute's No. 2 fairway.*

## GREENFIELD PARK GC

2028 S. 124th St. • West Allis 53227 • 414/453-1750

**Directions:** West on Greenfield to park entrance on 121st Street
**Course:** 18 holes/par 69/5,770 yards
**Fee:** $

This course is designed for the mid-handicap golfer. Wide fairways, low rough and moderately fast greens provide golfers with the right blend of challenge.

## HARTFORD GC

7072 Lee Rd. • Hartford 53027 • 414/673-2710

**Directions:** Hwy. 41 north to Hwy. 60 west 8 miles to Hartford, Hwy. 83 south two miles to Lee Road, west 1/2 mile on Lee Road
**Course:** 18 holes/par 72/6,411 yards
**Fee:** $$    Tee times required
**Amenities:** Driving range; full-service pro shop; Friday fish fry

This course is characterized by gentle, rolling terrain lined with many trees of different varieties and well-bunkered, challenging greens.

## HAWTHORNE HILLS GC

4720 Co. I • Saukville 53080 • 414/692-2151

**Directions**: I-43 to Hwy. 33 exit 96, west on Hwy. 33 to Co. I, three miles north
**Course:** 18 holes/par 72/6,595yards
**Fee:** $$
**Amenities:** Pro shop; restaurant; meeting room

This championship course is located in a scenic, rural setting. It offers rolling hills, mature trees and challenging water hazards.

## HEARTLAND HILLS GC

903 Madison Ave. • Howards Grove 53083 • 414/565-3674

**Directions:** Four miles northwest of I-43, exit 128
**Course:** 9 holes/par 34/2,479 yards
**Fee:** $
**Amenities:** Pro shop; clubhouse; bar

## HILLMOOR GC

Hwy. 50 East • P.O. Box 186 • Lake Geneva 53147 • 414/248-4570

**Directions:** On Hwy. 50 along the east edge of Lake Geneva
**Course:** 18 holes/par 72/6,318 yards
**Fee:** $$$    Carts required on weekends before 2 p.m.

**Amenities:** Driving range; putting green; breakfast and lunch daily; lessons; fully-stocked golf shop

Since 1924, golfers have enjoyed the rolling terrain around the White River. This uniquely designed course offers fun and challenge for golfers of all abilities.

# HON-E-KOR CC

1141 Riverview Dr. • Kewaskum 53040 • 414/626-2520

**Directions:** Located off Hwy. 28 on Riverview Drive South in Kewaskum
**Course:** 27 holes/par 35/3,017 yards, par 35/2,746 yards, par 35/2,660 yards
**Fee:** $$
**Amenities:** Pro shop; restaurant; corporate outings

Located in the heart of the beautiful and scenic Kettle Moraine, this course is a pretty one to play.

# IVES GROVE GL

14101 Washington Ave. • Sturtevant 53177 • 414/878-3714

**Directions:** One-quarter mile west of I-94 on Hwy. 20
**Course:** 18 holes/par 72/6,915 yards
**Fee:** $$
**Amenities:** Concession area; golf shop; outings available

This newer course sports watered fairways and has well-trapped greens to test your skills.

*The Trevino Course at Geneva National Golf Course*

*Blackwolf Run at Kohler*

## JOHNSON PARK GC

6200 Northwestern Ave. • Racine 53406 • 414/637-2840

**Directions:** Hwy. 38 just west of Racine
**Course:** 18 holes/par 72/6,683 yards
**Fee:** $$
**Amenities:** Pro shop

## KENOSHA MUNICIPAL

2205 Washington Rd. • Kenosha 53140 • 414/653-4090

**Directions:** I-94 to Washington
**Fee:** $

## KETTLE HILLS GC

3375 Hwy. 167 West • Richfield 53076-9603 • 414/628-0200 or 414/255-2200

**Directions:** Hwy. 41/45 north of Milwaukee to Hwy. 167 (Holy Hill Road), 1 1/2 miles west
**Course:** 27 holes/par 36/3,419 yards, par 36/3,368 yards, par 36/3,321 yards
**Fee:** $$    Tee times required
**Amenities:** Clubhouse; bar; pro shop; outing facilities with separate bar; two driving ranges; putting greens; practice tee, fairway and green with lessons available

On this course, beautiful native trees outline Kentucky bluegrass fairways with sand and grass berms to challenge golfers. Bentgrass greens can be found at each hole. A 60-foot drop into the Valley Course leads to open fairways outlined with wildflowers.

## KETTLE MORAINE GC

4299 Hwy. 67 • Dousman 53118 • 414/965-6200

**Directions:** On Hwy. 67, 7 1/2 miles south of I-94, 35 minutes north of Lake Geneva
**Course:** 18 holes/par 72/6,420 yards
**Fee:** $$$
**Amenities:** Clubhouse; banquet facilities

## KOSHKONONG MOUNDS CC

W7670 Koshkonong Mounds Rd. • Fort Atkinson 53538 • 414/563-2823

**Directions:** 3 1/2 miles south of Fort Atkinson, one mile west on Old Hwy. 26, then west on Koshkonong Mounds Road
**Course:** 18 holes/par 71/6,259 yards
**Fee:** $$

## LAKE BEULAH CC

N9430 East Shore Dr. • Mukwonago 53149 • 414/363-8147

**Directions:** Three miles southwest of Mukwonago on Co. J, 20 minutes from Milwaukee via I-43
**Course:** 18 holes/par 71/6,050 yards
**Fee:** $$
**Amenities:** Bar; pro shop; food

This beautifully landscaped course was built in two stages—one nine around 1920, the other around 1963. Now, a third nine is being added for a total of 27 holes. There are enough trees and water to make it an interesting round.

## LAKE LAWN LODGE GC

Hwy. 50 East, 2400 E. Geneva • Delavan 53115 • 414/728-7950

**Directions:** One mile east of I-43 on Hwy. 50
**Course:** 18 holes/par 70/6,418 yards
**Fee:** $$$$    Cart required at all times, tee times required two days in advance
**Amenities:** Hotel; extensive meeting facilities; resort; driving range

Since a redesign by architect Dick Nugent, Lake Lawn features well-bunkered, undulating bentgrass greens, breathtaking lake views and mature oak-lined fairways. Extensive use of berms and mounding gives the course somewhat of a Scottish look.

## LAKE PARK GC

N112 W17300 Mequon Rd. • Germantown 53022 • 414/255-4200

**Directions:** One mile east of Hwy. 45, Lannon Road Mequon Road exit
**Course:** 27 holes/each par 36/3,420 yards/3,559 yards/3,222 yards
**Fee:** $$    Tee times required

Beautiful vistas characterize all three of the nine holes, but the new nine is especially noteworthy. It features an island hole and has a tough slope rating of 132. Seventy bunkers, plenty of trees and the Menomonee River come into play often.

## LAKESIDE GC

W287 N3192 Lakeside Rd. • Pewaukee 53072 • 414/691-4630

**Directions:** On Co. KE (North Shore Drive), two miles south of Hwy. 16
**Course:** 9 holes/par 34/2,751 yards
**Fee:** $
**Amenities:** Cocktail lounge; banquet facilities

## LAUDERDALE LAKES CC

Hwys. 12 and 67 • Elkhorn 53121 • 414/742-2454

**Directions:** On Hwys. 12 and 67, five miles north of Elkhorn
**Course:** 9 holes/par 35/3,029 yards
**Fee:** $$
**Amenities:** Restaurant; bar (limited)

## LINCOLN PARK GC

1200 W. Hampton • Glendale 53209 • 414/962-2400

**Directions:** Exit I-43 on Hampton west
**Course:** 9 holes/par 33/2,538 yards
**Fee:** $

## MAPLECREST CC

9401 18th St. • Kenosha 53144 • 414/859-2887

**Directions:** Exit I-94 east on Hwy. 142 to Co. H north, then left on Co. L
**Course:** 18 holes/par 70/6,500 yards
**Fee:** $$
**Amenities:**   Pro shop; restaurant

## MAYVILLE GC

325 S. German St. • P.O. Box 129 • Mayville 53050 • 414/387-2999

**Directions:** On the south end of Mayville, just off Hwy. 67
**Course:** 18 holes/par 71/6,173 yards
**Fee:** $    Tee times required
**Amenities:** Restaurant

# MEADOW SPRINGS GC

424 S. Sandborn Ave. • Jefferson 53549 • 414/674-9986

**Directions:** I-94 to Hwy. 26 through Jefferson, left on East Washington
**Course:** 9 holes/par 35/2,989 yards
**Fee:** $$
**Amenities:** Pro shop; restaurant; bar; clubhouse (closed Mondays); ladies locker room

# MEE-KWON PARK GC

Ozaukee County Municipal
6333 W. Bonniwell Rd. • Mequon 53092 • 414/242-1310

**Directions:** I-43 to exit 85 Mequon Road, west on Mequon Road to Hwy. 57, then north to Bonniwell Road
**Course:** 18 holes/par 70/6,185 yards
**Fee:** $$

# MOOR DOWNS GC

438 Prospect Ave. • Waukesha 53188 • 414/548-7821

**Directions:** On the northwest side of Waukesha, just west of the county courthouse
**Course:** 9 holes/par 34/2,728 yards
**Fee:** $$

This old course, built in 1915, was acquired by Waukesha County in 1972.

*The beautiful Kettle Moraine Golf Course*

## MUSKEGO LAKES CC

S100 W14020 Loomis Rd. (Hwy. 36) • Muskego 53150 • 414/425-6500

**Directions:** On Hwy. 36, 3 1/2 miles south of Hwy. 100
**Course:** 18 holes/par 71/6,498 yards
**Fee:** $$
**Amenities:** Full irrigation; golf range; locker and shower rooms; banquet rooms; four PGA professionals available

This course is a three-time recipient of the National Golf Federation's Public Golf Achievement Award.

## NAGA-WAUKEE GC

1897 Maple Ave. • Pewaukee 53072 • 414/367-2153

**Directions:** I-94 to exit 290, west on Frontage Road to Co. E, then north one-half mile
**Course:** 18 holes/par 72/6,722yards
**Fee:** $$$

## NEW BERLIN HILLS GC

13175 W. Graham St. • New Berlin 53151 • 414/782-5005

**Directions:** I-894 to Greenfield Avenue, west to 124th, south on 124th to Graham Street, west on Graham
**Course:** 18 holes/par 71/6,496 yards
**Fee:** $$

## NIPPERSINK CC

N1055 Tombeau Road • Genoa City 53128 • 414/279-6311

**Directions:** Ten miles southeast of Lake Geneva, off Hwy. 12 to Co. P, follow signs
**Course:** 18 holes/par 71/6,318 yards
**Fee:** $$    Cart required on weekends and holidays until 10 a.m., tee times required
**Amenities:** Accommodations; clubhouse; snack shop and bar; lake; beach; pool; tennis; exercise room; banquet facilities

## OAK HILLS GC

10360 S. Howell • Oak Creek 53154 • 414/762-9994

**Directions:** One mile south of Hwys. 100 and 38
**Course:** 9 holes/par 31/2,130 yards
**Fee:** $
**Amenities:** Pro shop

*Grand Geneva Resort & Spa*

## OAKGREEN GC & DR

N7405 N. Pioneer Rd. • Fond du Lac 54937-8830 • 414/922-2273

**Directions:** Hwy. 41 to Co. OO, east to North Pioneer Road, then north one-quarter mile
**Course:** 9 holes/par 29/1,505 yards
**Fee:** $

## OAKWOOD GC

3720 W. Oakwood Rd. • Franklin 53132 • 414/281-6700

**Directions:** South on 27th Street, then west on Oakwood Road
**Course:** 18 holes/par 72/6,972 yards
**Fee:** $$
**Amenities:** Pro shop

This long course is characterized by large greens and fairways that are somewhat open.

## OLD HICKORY CC

W7596 Hwy. 33 East • Beaver Dam 53916 • 414/887-7577

**Directions:** 2 1/2 miles east of Beaver Dam on Hwy. 33
**Course:** 18 holes/par 72/6,667 yards
**Fee:** $$$
**Amenities:** Pro shop; snack bar

This course has hosted numerous state events and will meet you with rolling hills and elevated, fast greens.

## OLYMPIA RESORT GC

1350 Royale Mile Rd. • Oconomowoc 53066 • 414/567-2577

**Directions:** Exit I-94 on to Hwy. 67 North (exit 282), one mile north to the left. Sports center and pro shop at foot of ski hill on resort property.
**Course:** 18 holes/par 72/6,458 yards
**Fee:** $$$     Cart required on weekends
**Amenities:** Driving range; putting green; pro shop; rentals & lessons available

This resort course has undulating fairways, a variety of water hazards, tree-framed greens and three tees to choose from.

## PAGANICA GC

3850 Silver Lake • Oconomowoc 53066 • 414/567-0171

**Directions:** Take I-94 to Hwy. 67, north to Co. B, west 1 1/2 miles to Co. Z, north one-half mile
**Course:** 18 holes/par 72/6,678 yards
**Fee:** $$     Tee times required

## PETRIFYING SPRINGS GC

4909 7th St. • Kenosha 53144 • 414/552-9052

**Directions:** One block east of Hwy. 31 on Co. A
**Course:** 18 holes/par 71/5,970 yards
**Fee:** $$
**Amenities:** Snack bar

## QUIT-QUI-OC GC

500 Quit-Qui-Oc Ln. • Elkhart Lake 53020 • 414/876-2833

**Directions:** Hwy. 67 and Co. AJ, three miles east of Hwy. 57 in Sheboygan County
**Course:** 18 holes/par 70/6,154 yards
**Fee:** $$     Tee times required
**Amenities:** Restaurant; lounge; golf shop; driving range

This hilly course was initially built in 1925 then redone in 1959. New bunkers and tees and aggressive tree-planting have made this a worthy test of golf.

## RAINBOW SPRINGS GC

S103 W33599 Hwy. 99 • Mukwonago 53149 • 414/363-4550

**Directions:** Thirty miles west of Milwaukee's Mitchell Field airport,

1 1/2 hours north of Chicago
**Course:** 36 holes/par 72/7,135 yards, par 65/4,850 yards
**Fee:** $$$     (Fee includes cart)
**Amenities:** Bar; grill; pro shop; PGA member; professional staff

Rainbow Springs championship course has no bunkers and is one of the more unique, yet challenging, courses in the state. The executive course has junior as well as adult tees.

# RIVERDALE CC

5008 S. 12th St. • Sheboygan 53081 • 414/458-2561

**Directions:** I-43, exit on Co. V east to dead end, left two miles
**Course:** 18 holes/par 70/5,875 yards
**Fee:** $$     Weekend tee times required
**Amenities:** Driving range; fully stocked pro shop; lunch and dinner served

This well-maintained and manicured course offers a sporty layout for golfers.

# RIVERMOOR CC

30802 Waterford Dr. • Waterford 53185 • 414/534-2500

**Directions:** On Hwys. 20 and 83 at west edge of village, eight miles south of I-43
**Course:** 18 holes/par 70/6,256 yards
**Fee:** $$
**Amenities:** Lunch and dinner served; weekend snack bar and beverage cart

*Abbey Springs Golf Course in Fontana*

## RIVERSBEND GC

N96 W18034 County Line Rd. • Germantown 53022 • 414/255-6557

**Directions:** Hwy. 41/45 to Co. Q west
**Course:** 9 holes/par 33/2,300 yards
**Fee:** $
**Amenities:** Pro shop; snack bar

## ROCK RIVER HILLS

Main Street Road • P.O. Box 56 • Horicon 53032 • 414/485-4990

**Directions:** Hwy. 33 into Horicon, then proceed on Main Street Road about one mile
**Course:** 18 holes/par 70/6,265 yards
**Fee:** $$
**Amenities:** Full-service pro shop; clubhouse; dining facilities

This course, built along the Rock River, features water on 13 of its 18 holes. It is picturesque and often referred to as a target golf course that presents the experienced golfer with rich rewards for accurate shots and disaster for errant shots.

## ROLLING MEADOWS GC

560 W. Rolling Meadows Dr. • Fond du Lac 54937 • 414/929-3735

**Directions:** From Hwy. 151, one-quarter mile south on Rolling Meadows Drive
**Course:** 9 holes/par 35/3,050 yards
**Fee:** $$    Tee times required

Scheduled to have 27 holes in mid-1995, this course is set on rolling terrain. It's characterized by many sand and grass bunkers. Ample water and length add challenge.

## ST. JOHN'S MILITARY ACADEMY GC

1101 N. Genesee St. • Delafield 53018 • 414/646-3311

**Directions:** North of I-94 and west of Co. C
**Course:** 9 holes/par 36/3,152 yards
**Fee:** $$

## SCENIC VIEW CC

4415 Club Dr. • Slinger 53086 • 800/472-6411

**Directions:** On Co. J, 3 1/2 miles north of Hwy. 167 and two miles south of Hwy. 60.

**Course:** 18 holes/par 72/6,223 yards
**Fee:** $$
**Amenities:** Driving range; snack bar; restaurant; banquet facilities; locker room facilities

In the heart of the Kettle Moraine area, this course lives up to its name with numerous overlooks into a beautiful valley.

## SHEBOYGAN TOWN & COUNTRY

W1945 Co. J • Sheboygan 53083 • 414/467-2509

**Directions:** I-43 north to Sheboygan exit 128, southeast two blocks, then right on Co. J, west two miles
**Course:** 27 holes, each par 36/2,664 yards/3,124 yards/3,139 yards
**Fee:** $$
**Amenities:** Golf range; lounge; restaurant; lessons

## SHOOP PARK GC

Co. G • Racine 53405 • 414/681-9714

**Directions:** Four Mile Road east to Lake Michigan
**Course:** 9 holes/par 34/2,631 yards
**Fee:** $

## SILVER SPRING CC

N56 W21318 W. Silver Spring • Menomonee Falls 53051 • 414/252-4666

**Directions:** On Silver Spring Drive 5 1/2 miles west of Hwys. 100 and 45.
**Course:** 27 holes, each par 36/3,148 yards/3,099 yards/3,199 yards
**Fee:** $$$    Tee times required
**Amenities:** Two-level driving range; full-service restaurant; banquet facilities; locker room facilities; lounge; snack bar

This rapidly expanding course north of Milwaukee is working on nine more holes for 1995. The holes are set in the rolling hills of Waukesha County. A Fox River tributary flows through the course, challenging players on six holes. Ponds, fairway bunkers and aged willows add to the course's natural beauty. One key feature: Wisconsin's only natural island hole.

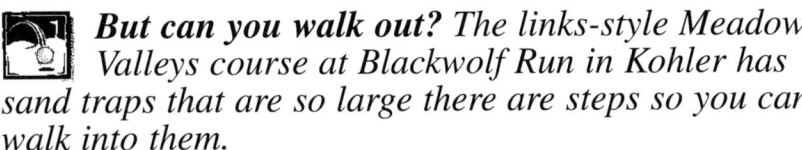

*But can you walk out? The links-style Meadow Valleys course at Blackwolf Run in Kohler has sand traps that are so large there are steps so you can walk into them.*

## SONGBIRD HILLS GC

W259 N8700 Hwy. J • Hartland 53029 • 414/246-7050

**Directions:** Four miles northwest of Sussex. About 9 1/2 miles north of I-94
**Course:** 18 holes/par 70/5,541 yards
**Fee:** $$
**Amenities:** Large party pavilion; new power carts; group & private lessons

## SOUTH HILLS CC

3047 Hwy. 41 • Franksville 53126 • 414/835-4441

**Directions:** I-94 to Frontage Road, between Co. K and Hwy. 20
**Course:** 18 holes/par 72/6,403 yards
**Fee:** $$
**Amenities:** Banquet facilities

## SPRING VALLEY CC

23913 Wilmot Rd. • Salem 53168 • 414/862-2626

**Directions:** Eight miles west of I-94 on Co. C at Hwy. 83, two miles north of Antioch, Ill.
**Course:** 18 holes/par 70/6,272 yards
**Fee:** $$    Tee times required
**Amenities:** Full-service bar with lunch served daily and dinner served Fridays

Built in 1924, this hilly course has a large number of mature trees and many grass bunkers but no sand. Water comes into play on four holes. Elevated tees and greens plus a double-row irrigation system improve the natural surroundings.

## THE SQUIRES GC

4970 Country Club Rd. • Port Washington 53074 • 414/285-3402

**Directions:** 3 1/2 miles north of Port Washington on Co. LL
**Course:** 18 holes/par 70/5,800 yards
**Fee:** $$
**Amenities:** Practice range; complete pro shop; sandwiches at grill; banquet facilities

This well-groomed course, built in two stages (1927 and 1958), features beautiful views of Lake Michigan.

## SUNSET HILLS GOLF & SUPPER CLUB

Hwy. 33 • Beaver Dam 53916 • 414/885-6614

**Directions:** Hwy. 151 to Industrial Drive, west to DeClark Street, north to Hwy. 33, 2 1/2 miles north of city
**Course:** 18 holes/par 72/5,913 yards
**Fee:** $$

## TRENTON VIEW

1241 Hwy. 33 East • West Bend 53095 • 414/675-6669
**Directions:** Four miles east of West Bend on Hwy. 33
**Course:** 9 holes/par 36/3,276 yards
**Fee:** $$
**Amenities:** Horseshoes; batting cages; sand volleyball; softball diamond

## TWIN LAKES CC

1230 Legion Dr. • Twin Lakes 53181 • 414/877-2500
**Directions:** Ten miles southeast of Lake Geneva near Illinois border
**Course:** 18 holes/par 70/6,020 yards
**Fee:** $$

## TYRANENA GC

800 S. Main St. • Lake Mills 53551 • 414/648-5013
**Directions:** 1 1/2 miles south of I-94 on Hwy. 89
**Course:** 9 holes/par 35/3,010 yards
**Fee:** $$    Tee times required on weekends and holidays

This old course (built in 1926) has undergone much revision—three new holes in the past two years—yet has maintained its old-course feel. This mature course has more than 5,000 pine trees. A new nine being added will have four water holes.

## WANAKI GC

N50 W20830 Lisbon Rd. • Menomonee Falls 53051 • 414/252-3480
**Directions:** Two miles east of Hwy. 164, junction of Co. K and Co. Y
**Course:** 18 holes/par 70/6,500 yards
**Fee:** $$

This Waukesha County course was built in 1970.

## WASHINGTON PARK GC

2801 12th St. • Racine 53405 • 414/635-0118
**Directions:** Hwy. 20 east to 12th Street
**Course:** 9 holes/par 35/2,690 yards
**Fee:** $
**Amenities:** Practice green; clubhouse

*Rainbow Springs Golf Course in Mukwonago*

## WESTERN LAKES GC

W287 N1963 Oakton Rd. • Pewaukee 53072 • 414/691-1181

**Directions:** I-94 to Co. SS north about three blocks, then turn left on Oakton Road
**Course:** 18 holes/par 72/6,573 yards
**Fee:** $$$    Tee times required
**Amenities:** Practice facilities; full-service pro shop; banquet and meeting rooms; sandwiches

Designed in 1962 by Lawrence Packard, this course has 36 traps and ample water, which comes into play on 13 holes.

## WHISPERING SPRINGS

1646 Golf Course Dr. • Fond du Lac 54935 • 414/921-8053

**Directions:** Hwy. 41 to Hwy. 23 east, ten miles to Co. UU, left on UU, then left on Co. A
**Course:** 9 holes/par 36/3,094 yards
**Fee:** Unavailable at time of printing

Course will not open until 1995.

## WHITNALL GC

5879 S. 92nd St. • Hales Corners 53130 • 414/425-7931

**Directions:** Hwy. 100 south to Rawson Avenue, east on Rawson, then left on 92nd Street
**Course:** 18 holes/par 71/6,216 yards
**Fee:** $$
**Amenities:**  Pro shop; restaurant; golf range

This scenic course has many large, old trees providing challenge to all player levels.

# WILLOW RUN GC

N12 W26506 Golf Rd. • Pewaukee 53072 • 414/544-8585

**Directions:** I-94 to Co. T north, west on Golf Road one-half mile, adjacent to the Country Inn Hotel and Conference Center
**Course:** 18 holes/par 71/6,400 yards
**Fee:** $$
**Amenities:** Complete pro shop; clubhouse; restaurant; full practice facilities with instructors; group meeting facilities; banquet facility

This low-lying course, built in 1960, has water on 14 of its 18 holes. Four sets of tees provide variety.

# WOODLAND GC

3025 E. Elm Road • Oak Creek 53154 • 414/762-1101

**Directions:** One mile west of Hwy. 32 on Elm Road, southeastern corner of Milwaukee County
**Course:** 9 holes/par 31/2,107 yards
**Fee:** $

# Golf Course Index

| | Page |
|---|---|
| ABBEY SPRINGS GOLF COURSE | 1, 136 |
| ALASKAN GOLF COURSE | 86 |
| ALPINE GOLF COURSE | 86 |
| ALPINE VALLEY RESORT | 136 |
| AMERICAN LEGION GOLF COURSE | 86 |
| AMERY GOLF COURSE | 66 |
| ANTIGO BASS LAKE | 86 |
| APOSTLE HIGHLANDS | 66 |
| ARCADIA GOLF COURSE | 114 |
| ARROWHEAD SPRINGS | 136 |
| AUBURN BLUFF GOLF COURSE | 136 |
| | |
| BARABOO COUNTRY CLUB | 114 |
| BARKER LAKE COUNTRY LODGE & GOLF COURSE | 66 |
| BAY RIDGE GOLF COURSE | 87 |
| BIG OAKS GOLF COURSE | 136 |
| BIG SAND GOLF COURSE | 87 |
| BIG STONE GOLF COURSE & COUNTRY CLUB | 87 |
| BIRCHWOOD GOLF & DEVELOPMENT | 114 |
| BLACK RIVER COUNTRY CLUB | 66 |
| BLACKHAWK GOLF COURSE | 114 |
| BLACKWOLF RUN | 4, 136 |
| BLOOMER MEMORIAL GOLF COURSE | 67 |
| BOMBERS BAR & GOLF | 87 |
| BONNY MEADE LINKS | 114 |
| BOTTEN'S GREEN ACRES GOLF COURSE | 67 |
| BRIDGEWOOD GOLF COURSE | 87 |
| BRIGHTON DALE LINKS | 137 |
| BRISTOL OAKS COUNTRY CLUB | 137 |
| BRISTOL RIDGE GOLF COURSE | 67 |
| BROOKFIELD HILLS GOLF COURSE | 137 |
| BROWN COUNTY GOLF COURSE | 7, 88 |
| BROWN DEER GOLF COURSE | 10, 138 |
| BROWN'S LAKE GOLF COURSE | 138 |
| BUTTERNUT HILLS GOLF COURSE | 68 |
| | |
| CAMELOT COUNTRY CLUB | 138 |
| CASTLE ROCK GOLF COURSE | 115 |
| CECELIA'S GOLF COURSE | 115 |
| CEDAR SPRINGS GOLF COURSE | 88 |
| CHABRE GOLF COURSE | 68 |
| CHASKA GOLF COURSE | 88 |

| | Page |
|---|---|
| CHERRY HILLS GOLF COURSE | 88 |
| CHRISTMAS MOUNTAIN RESORT | 115 |
| CLEAR LAKE GOLF COURSE | 68 |
| CLIFTON HIGHLANDS GOLF COURSE | 68 |
| CLIFTON HOLLOW GOLF COURSE | 69 |
| CLINTONVILLE RIVERSIDE GOLF COURSE | 88 |
| COACHMAN'S INN COUNTRY CLUB | 115 |
| COLDWATER CANYON GOLF COURSE | 116 |
| COLE ACRES GOLF COURSE & SUPPER CLUB | 116 |
| COULEE GOLF BOWL | 116 |
| COUNTRY CLUB ESTATES | 138 |
| COUNTRY CLUB OF WISCONSIN | 138 |
| COUNTRY SIDE GOLF CLUB | 88 |
| CRANE MEADOWS GOLF COURSE | 89 |
| CRYSTAL LAKE GOLF COURSE | 139 |
| CRYSTAL SPRINGS GOLF COURSE | 89 |
| CUMBERLAND GOLF COURSE | 69 |
| CURRIE PARK GOLF COURSE | 139 |
| | |
| DARLINGTON COUNTRY CLUB | 116 |
| DECATUR LAKE COUNTRY CLUB | 117 |
| DEER RUN COUNTRY CLUB | 89 |
| DEERTRAK GOLF COURSE | 139 |
| DELBROOK GOLF COURSE | 139 |
| DELL VIEW GOLF COURSE | 117 |
| DESMIDT'S GOLF COURSE & COUNTRY CLUB | 90 |
| DEVIL'S HEAD LODGE | 13, 118 |
| DODGE POINT COUNTRY CLUB | 118 |
| DOOR CREEK GOLF COURSE | 118 |
| DRETZKA PARK GOLF COURSE | 139 |
| DRUGAN'S CASTLE MOUND | 118 |
| DURAND GOLF COURSE | 118 |
| | |
| EAGLE BLUFF GOLF COURSE | 69 |
| EAGLE RIVER MUNI GOLF COURSE | 90 |
| EAGLE SPRINGS GOLF RESORT | 140 |
| EDELWEISS CHALET COUNTRY CLUB | 119 |
| EDGEWATER, GRAFTON | 140 |
| EDGEWATER GOLF COURSE, TOMAHAWK | 90 |
| EDGEWOOD GOLF COURSE, BIG BEND | 140 |
| EDGEWOOD GOLF COURSE, OCONTO | 90 |
| ELKS COUNTRY CLUB, ASHLAND | 69 |
| ELKS COUNTRY CLUB, CHIPPEWA FALLS | 70 |
| ELLSWORTH COUNTRY CLUB | 70 |
| ETTRICK GOLF COURSE | 119 |
| EVANSVILLE GOLF COURSE | 119 |

*Great Golf in Wisconsin*

| | Page |
|---|---|
| EVERGREEN COUNTRY CLUB | 140 |
| | |
| FAIRVIEW GOLF COURSE | 90 |
| FAR VU GOLF COURSE | 91 |
| FIVE FLAGS COUNTRY CLUB | 70 |
| FOREST POINT GOLF COURSE | 70 |
| FOUR SEASONS GOLF COURSE | 91 |
| FOX HILLS RESORT | 91 |
| FOX LAKE GOLF COURSE | 140 |
| FOXBORO GOLF COURSE | 119 |
| FREDERIC COUNTRY CLUB | 70 |
| | |
| GATEWAY GOLF COURSE | 91 |
| GENEVA NATIONAL GOLF CLUB | 16, 141 |
| GEORGE WILLIAMS COLLEGE GOLF COURSE | 141 |
| GLEN CAIRN GOLF COURSE | 92 |
| GLEN HILLS GOLF COURSE | 70 |
| GLENWAY GOLF COURSE | 120 |
| GOLDEN SANDS GOLF COURSE | 92 |
| GRAND GENEVA RESORT & SPA | 19, 141 |
| GRANDVIEW GOLF COURSE | 92 |
| GRANT PARK GOLF COURSE | 141 |
| GRANTSBURG MUNICIPAL GOLF COURSE | 71 |
| GREEN ACRES | 92 |
| GREENFIELD PARK GOLF COURSE | 142 |
| GREENWOOD HILLS COUNTRY CLUB | 92 |
| | |
| HALLIE GOLF COURSE | 71 |
| HAMMOND GOLF COURSE | 71 |
| HARTFORD GOLF COURSE | 142 |
| HAWTHORNE HILLS GOLF COURSE | 142 |
| HAYWARD GOLF & TENNIS CLUB | 72 |
| HEARTLAND HILLS GOLF COURSE | 142 |
| HIAWATHA GOLF COURSE | 120 |
| HICKORY GROVE GOLF COURSE | 120 |
| HICKORY HILLS GOLF COURSE | 93 |
| HIGH CLIFF GOLF COURSE | 93 |
| HIGHLAND RIDGE GOLF COURSE | 93 |
| HILLMOOR GOLF COURSE | 142 |
| HILLY HAVEN SKI & GOLF | 93 |
| HOLIDAY LODGE GOLF RESORT & SUPPER CLUB | 121 |
| HOMESTEAD GOLF COURSE | 94 |
| HON-E-KOR COUNTRY CLUB | 143 |
| HUDSON COUNTRY CLUB | 72 |
| | |
| IDLEWILD GOLF COURSE OF DOOR COUNTY | 94 |

|  | Page |
|---|---|
| INDIANHEAD GOLF COURSE | 94 |
| INSHALLA COUNTRY CLUB | 94 |
| IOLA COMMUNITY GOLF COURSE | 95 |
| IRISH WATERS GOLF COURSE | 95 |
| IVES GROVE GOLF LINKS | 143 |
| JOHNSON PARK GOLF COURSE | 144 |
| KENOSHA MUNICIPAL | 144 |
| KETTLE HILLS GOLF COURSE | 144 |
| KETTLE MORAINE GOLF COURSE | 145 |
| KOSHKONONG MOUNDS COUNTRY CLUB | 145 |
| KROOKED KREEK GOLF COURSE | 72 |
| KRUEGER MUNICIPAL GOLF COURSE | 121 |
| LAKE ARROWHEAD GOLF COURSE | 22, 95 |
| LAKE BEULAH COUNTRY CLUB | 145 |
| LAKE BREEZE GOLF COURSE | 95 |
| LAKE FOREST GOLF COURSE | 96 |
| LAKE LAWN LODGE GOLF COURSE | 145 |
| LAKE PARK GOLF COURSE | 146 |
| LAKE SHORE GOLF COURSE | 96 |
| LAKE WINDSOR COUNTRY CLUB | 121 |
| LAKE WISCONSIN COUNTRY CLUB | 121 |
| LAKELAND HILLS COUNTRY CLUB | 122 |
| LAKESIDE GOLF COURSE | 146 |
| LAKEWOODS FOREST RIDGES GOLF COURSE | 72 |
| LANCASTER COUNTRY CLUB | 122 |
| LAUDERDALE LAKES COUNTRY CLUB | 146 |
| LAWSONIA | 25, 122 |
| LINCOLN PARK GOLF COURSE | 146 |
| LITTLE RIVER COUNTRY CLUB | 96 |
| LUCK GOLF COURSE | 72 |
| LUDDEN LAKE GOLF COURSE | 122 |
| MACDONALD'S RIVER BEND | 122 |
| MADELINE ISLAND GOLF COURSE | 28, 73 |
| MAPLE GROVE COUNTRY CLUB | 123 |
| MAPLE GROVE GOLF COURSE & RESORT | 96 |
| MAPLE HILLS GOLF COURSE | 96 |
| MAPLE VALLEY GOLF COURSE | 97 |
| MAPLECREST COUNTRY CLUB | 146 |
| MAPLEWOOD GOLF COURSE | 97 |
| MARSHFIELD COUNTRY CLUB | 98 |
| MASCOUTIN GOLF CLUB | 31, 123 |
| MAXWELTON BRAES GOLF COURSE | 98 |

| | Page |
|---|---|
| MAYVILLE GOLF COURSE | 146 |
| MCCAUSLIN BROOK GOLF COURSE | 98 |
| MEADOW LINKS GOLF COURSE | 99 |
| MEADOW SPRINGS GOLF COURSE | 147 |
| MEADOWVIEW GOLF COURSE | 73 |
| MEE-KWON PARK GOLF COURSE | 147 |
| MELLEN COUNTRY CLUB | 73 |
| MENOMONIE GOLF & COUNTRY CLUB | 74 |
| MERRILL GOLF COURSE | 99 |
| MID-VALLEE GOLF COURSE | 99 |
| MILL RUN GOLF COURSE | 74 |
| MINOCQUA COUNTRY CLUB | 99 |
| MONONA GOLF COURSE | 123 |
| MOOR DOWNS GOLF COURSE | 147 |
| MOUNDVIEW GOLF COURSE | 123 |
| MUSKEGO LAKES COUNTRY CLUB | 148 |
| MYSTERY HILLS GOLF COURSE | 99 |
| | |
| NAGA-WAUKEE GOLF COURSE | 34, 148 |
| NEILLSVILLE GOLF COURSE | 74 |
| NEMADJI GOLF COURSE | 74 |
| NEW BERLIN HILLS GOLF COURSE | 148 |
| NEW LONDON GOLF COURSE | 100 |
| NEW RICHMOND GOLF COURSE | 37, 75 |
| NICOLET COUNTRY CLUB | 100 |
| NINE SPRINGS GOLF COURSE | 124 |
| NIPPERSINK COUNTRY CLUB | 148 |
| NORSK GOLF BOWL | 124 |
| NORTHBROOK COUNTRY CLUB | 100 |
| NORTHWOOD GOLF COURSE | 40, 100 |
| NORWOOD GOLF COURSE | 75 |
| | |
| OAK HILLS GOLF COURSE | 148 |
| OAK RIDGE GOLF COURSE | 124 |
| OAKGREEN GOLF COURSE & DRIVING RANGE | 149 |
| OAKWOOD GOLF COURSE | 149 |
| OCONTO GOLF COURSE | 100 |
| ODANA HILLS GOLF COURSE | 124 |
| OJIBWA GOLF AND BOWL | 75 |
| OLD HICKORY COUNTRY CLUB | 43, 149 |
| OLYMPIA RESORT GOLF COURSE | 150 |
| OSSEO GOLF COURSE | 124 |
| | |
| PAGANICA GOLF COURSE | 150 |
| PARK FALLS GOLF COURSE | 76 |
| PATTISON PARK GOLF COURSE | 76 |

|  | Page |
|---|---|
| PECK'S WILDWOOD GOLF COURSE | 101 |
| PENINSULA STATE PARK GOLF COURSE | 46, 101 |
| PETRIFYING SPRINGS GOLF COURSE | 150 |
| PINE ACRES GOLF COURSE | 101 |
| PINE CREST GOLF | 76 |
| PINE HILLS COUNTRY CLUB | 101 |
| PINE VALLEY GOLF COURSE | 102 |
| PINEWOOD COUNTRY CLUB | 102 |
| PLATTEVILLE GOLF & COUNTRY CLUB | 125 |
| PLEASANT VIEW GOLF COURSE | 125 |
| PLUM LAKE GOLF COURSE | 102 |
| POPLAR GOLF & RECREATION AREA | 76 |
| PORTAGE COUNTRY CLUB | 125 |
| PRAIRIE DU CHIEN COUNTRY CLUB | 125 |
| PRENTICE VILLAGE GOLF COURSE | 76 |
| PRINCETON VALLEY GOLF COURSE | 76 |
|  |  |
| QUAIL RUN GOLF LINKS | 126 |
| QUIT-QUI-OC GOLF COURSE | 150 |
|  |  |
| RAINBOW RIDGE GOLF COURSE | 77 |
| RAINBOW SPRINGS GOLF COURSE | 49, 150 |
| REEDSBURG COUNTRY CLUB | 126 |
| REID MUNICIPAL GOLF COURSE | 102 |
| RIB MOUNTAIN GOLF COURSE | 103 |
| RIDGES GOLF COURSE, THE | 103 |
| RIVER FALLS GOLF COURSE | 77 |
| RIVER ISLAND GOLF COURSE | 103 |
| RIVERDALE COUNTRY CLUB | 151 |
| RIVEREDGE COUNTRY CLUB | 103 |
| RIVERMOOR COUNTRY CLUB | 151 |
| RIVERSBEND GOLF COURSE | 152 |
| RIVERSIDE GOLF COURSE | 126 |
| RIVERVIEW COUNTRY CLUB & GOLF COURSE | 104 |
| ROCK RIVER HILLS | 152 |
| ROLLING MEADOWS GOLF COURSE | 152 |
| ROLLING OAKS GOLF COURSE | 77 |
| ROYAL SCOT GOLF COURSE | 104 |
| ROYNONA CREEK GOLF COURSE | 78 |
|  |  |
| ST. CROIX VALLEY COUNTRY CLUB | 78 |
| ST. GERMAIN GOLF COURSE | 104 |
| ST. JOHN'S MILITARY ACADEMY GOLF COURSE | 152 |
| SANDALWOOD COUNTRY CLUB | 104 |
| SCENIC VIEW COUNTRY CLUB | 152 |
| SENTRYWORLD | 52, 104 |

| | Page |
|---|---|
| SHAWANO LAKE GOLF COURSE | 105 |
| SHEBOYGAN TOWN & COUNTRY | 153 |
| SHOOP PARK GOLF COURSE | 153 |
| SHOREWOOD | 105 |
| SILVER SPRING COUNTRY CLUB | 153 |
| SKYLINE GOLF COURSE | 126 |
| SONGBIRD HILLS GOLF COURSE | 154 |
| SOUTH HILLS COUNTRY CLUB | 154 |
| SPARTA MUNICIPAL GOLF COURSE | 127 |
| SPIDER LAKE COUNTRY CLUB | 78 |
| SPOONER GOLF COURSE | 78 |
| SPREAD EAGLE GOLF COURSE | 105 |
| SPRING GREEN GOLF COURSE | 127 |
| SPRING VALLEY COUNTRY CLUB | 154 |
| SPRING VALLEY GOLF COURSE, SPRING VALLEY | 78 |
| SPRING VALLEY COLF COURSE, UNION CENTER | 127 |
| SPRINGS GOLF CLUB RESORT, THE | 55, 127 |
| SQUIRES GOLF COURSE, THE | 154 |
| STONEHEDGE GOLF COURSE | 106 |
| SUNDOWN GOLF COURSE | 106 |
| SUN PRAIRIE COUNTRY CLUB | 128 |
| SUNSET HILLS GOLF & SUPPER CLUB | 154 |
| SUNSET VIEW COUNTRY CLUB | 79 |
| SWAN LAKE VILLAGE GOLF COURSE | 128 |
| | |
| TAGALONG GOLF COURSE | 79 |
| TAHKODAH HILLS GOLF COURSE | 79 |
| TAYLOR'S AMACOY GOLF & SUPPER CLUB | 80 |
| TEE-A-WAY GOLF & SUPPER CLUB | 80 |
| TEE-HI CLUB | 80 |
| TELEMARK GOLF COURSE | 80 |
| THAL ACRES LINKS & LANES | 128 |
| THORNBERRY CREEK COUNTRY CLUB | 106 |
| TIMBER TERRACE GOLF COURSE | 80 |
| TOWNE COUNTRY CLUB | 128 |
| TRAPP RIVER GOLF COURSE | 106 |
| TRAPPERS TURN GOLF COURSE | 58, 128 |
| TREE ACRES GOLF COURSE | 106 |
| TRENTON VIEW | 155 |
| TRI-CITY GOLF COURSE | 107 |
| TROUT LAKE GOLF & COUNTRY CLUB | 107 |
| TUMBLEDOWN TRAILS GOLF COURSE | 129 |
| TURTLE GREENS GOLF COURSE | 129 |
| TURTLEBACK GOLF & COUNTRY CLUB | 81 |
| TUSCUMBIA GOLF COURSE | 129 |
| TWIN LAKES COUNTRY CLUB | 155 |

|  | Page |
|---|---|
| TWIN OAKS COUNTRY CLUB | 108 |
| TWO OAKS NORTH | 130 |
| TYRANENA GOLF COURSE | 155 |
| UNIVERSITY RIDGE GOLF COURSE | 61, 130 |
| UTICA GOLF COURSE | 108 |
| VALLEY, THE | 130 |
| VIKING SKYLINE GOLF | 131 |
| VILLAGE GREEN GOLF COURSE | 108 |
| VOYAGER VILLAGE COUNTRY CLUB | 81 |
| WALNUT GROVE GOLF COURSE | 131 |
| WALSH GOLF COURSE | 131 |
| WANAKI GOLF COURSE | 155 |
| WANDER SPRINGS | 108 |
| WASHINGTON PARK GOLF COURSE | 155 |
| WAUSHARA COUNTRY CLUB | 131 |
| WEDGEWOOD SUPPER CLUB & GOLF COURSE | 109 |
| WESTBROOK HILLS GOLF COURSE | 132 |
| WESTHAVEN GOLF COURSE | 109 |
| WESTERN LAKES GOLF COURSE | 156 |
| WESTWOOD GOLF & SUPPER CLUB | 82 |
| WEYMONT RUN COUNTRY CLUB | 110 |
| WHISPERING PINES GOLF COURSE | 82 |
| WHISPERING SPRINGS | 156 |
| WHITE LAKE COUNTRY CLUB | 133 |
| WHITEHALL GOLF COURSE | 132 |
| WHITETAIL GOLF COURSE | 83 |
| WHITNALL GOLF COURSE | 156 |
| WILLOW RUN GOLF COURSE | 157 |
| WINAGAMIE GOLF COURSE | 110 |
| WINCHESTER HILLS GOLF COURSE | 110 |
| WINDY ACRES GOLF COURSE | 133 |
| WISCONSIN RIVER COUNTRY CLUB | 111 |
| WOODLAND GOLF COURSE | 157 |
| WOODSIDE COUNTRY CLUB | 111 |
| YAHARA HILLS GOLF COURSE | 133 |
| YELLOW LAKE GOLF COURSE | 83 |

 # Notes